GALÁPAGOS WILDLIFE

David Horwell
Pete Oxford

Bradt Travel Guides Ltd, UK
The Globe Pequot Press Inc, USA

Third edition August 2011
First published 1999
Bradt Travel Guides Ltd
IDC House, The Vale, Chalfont St Peter, Bucks SL9 9RZ, England
www.bradtguides.com
Published in the USA by
The Globe Pequot Press Inc
PO Box 480, Guilford, Connecticut 06437-0480

The authors and publishers have made every effort to ensure the accuracy
of the information in this book at the time of going to press.
However, the publishers cannot accept any responsibility for any loss,
injury or inconvenience resulting from the use of information contained in this guide.

British Library Cataloguing in Publication Data
A catalogue record for this book is available from the British Library

ISBN: 978 1 84162 360 3

Photographs
Hilary Bradt (HB), Jonathan R Green (JRG),
David Horwell (DH), Pete Oxford (PO), Tui de Roy/FLPA (TDR/FLPA)

Front cover, main image: Albatross (PO)
Front cover, inset images (left to right): Marine iguana (PO),
Frigatebird (TDR/FLPA), Sea lion (PO)
Back cover: Whale shark with tropical fish (PO)
Title page: Saddleback tortoise (PO)

Maps
Steve Munns, Alan Whitaker

Typeset and designed from the authors' disk by Artinfusion,
based on a design by Ian Chatterton
Production managed by Jellyfish Print Solutions
and manufactured in India

CONTENTS

An Introduction to the Galápagos	**1**
Habitats	**7**
Plants	**15**
Invertebrates	**27**
Reptiles	**33**
Tortoises	35
Turtles	41
Lizards and Snakes	43
Birds	**49**
Land Birds	51
Seabirds	58
Shore Birds	76
Mammals	**83**
Sea Lions	85
Whales and Dolphins	90
Land Mammals	92
The Seashore	**93**
Underwater	**97**
Bony Fishes	100
Sharks and Rays	103
Island Landings and Visitor Sites	**109**
Conservation	**141**
Glossary	**150**
Further Reading	**152**
Index	**153**

AUTHORS AND PHOTOGRAPHERS

David Horwell is a tour operator, photographer and writer who specialises in the Galápagos. A fellow of the Royal Geographical Society, his photographs have been published in magazines from *The Sunday Times* to *Wanderlust*. He has travelled extensively throughout South America, both alone and leading special-interest groups, and in 1978 became a licensed Galápagos guide. Based in Britain, David now runs Select Latin America (*www.selectlatinamerica.co.uk*), taking small groups to the Galápagos and Ecuador each year, and offers advice to independent travellers. He can be contacted by email at david@selectlatinamerica.co.uk.

Pete Oxford, a professional naturalist and photographer, first visited the Galápagos in 1985. He became a licensed guide in 1987, while living in Puerto Ayora on Santa Cruz. He continues to reside in Ecuador and still regularly visits the islands. He has worked in over 40 countries and visited many more. His photographs have appeared in all the major magazines in his field including *National Geographic*, *BBC Wildlife*, *Geo*, *International Wildlife* and *Smithsonian*. He regularly features in the *BBC Wildlife* Photographer of the Year competition. He has written ten books. Pete is a founding fellow of the International League of Conservation Photographers (*www.ilcp.com*). Pete can be contacted at pete@peteoxford.com.

Jonathan R Green is originally from England, where he graduated with a BSc Combined Science in Geology and Geography from North London University. He has lived in France and Spain and currently resides near Quito, in the Andes of Ecuador. He has spent many years working as a naturalist and dive guide in the Galápagos Islands, as well as leading adventure travel trips into the Amazon rainforest, Peru and Patagonia. He is a widely published photographer of both land and underwater photography. He can be contacted at PO Box 17-22-20288, Quito, Ecuador; email: jonathan@jonathangreenimages.com.

Hilary Bradt led eight trips to the Galápagos during the 1980s and published the first definitive map of the islands. She can be contacted via Bradt Travel Guides.

ACKNOWLEDGEMENTS
Thanks to Henri Herrera, entomologist at the Charles Darwin Research Station, and his colleagues Bernard Landry and Lazaro Roque-Albelo, for help with the updates for the new edition.

Pete Oxford wishes to thank Reneé Bish – with whom anything is possible.

AN INTRODUCTION TO THE GALÁPAGOS

T he Galápagos Archipelago encompasses a land area of approximately 8,000km² straddling the Equator between 1.5° north and 0.5° south, and spanning from 89° to 92° west. The nearest mainland belongs to Ecuador, which has sovereignty over the islands and lies 1,000km to the east. The archipelago consists of one major island, Isabela, which represents more than half the total land area, and six smaller islands of over 100km²: Santa Cruz, Fernandina, Santiago, San Cristóbal, Floreana and Marchena (in descending order of size). There are a further six small islands between 10 and 100km² and six more 1–10km² in size. There are also many smaller rocks and islets. Being volcanic in origin (see below), the rocks of the islands consist almost entirely of oceanic basalt. This forms lava, cinder or ash depending on the nature of the eruption.

GEOLOGY

The geography and geology of the Galápagos are vital to the biology of the islands. The Galápagos have never been attached to a mainland, but instead arose directly from the sea, being actually the tips of huge submarine volcanoes. This means that any life that has settled on the islands has arrived from some other, far-off source of colonisation. Once the red-hot lava of the new islands cooled to form rock, the sterile land masses were colonised little by little by the hardy plants and animals that arrived and managed to establish themselves.

The Galápagos Islands are situated on the confluence of three of the earth's tectonic plates – the Pacific, Cocos and Nazca plates. Tectonic plates are huge pieces of the earth's crust, bearing either continents or ocean floor, or both, which are floating on a bed of liquid rock or magma. In the Galápagos region, the three plates are pushed apart by convection currents caused by heat deep inside the earth, with the result that the Galápagos archipelago, sitting on the Nazca plate, is drifting in a southeasterly direction at the rate of about seven centimetres a year.

The age of the islands increases sequentially from west to east with the southeasternmost island, Española, being the oldest. Fernandina to the west is the youngest of the archipelago – less than 700,000 years old. To explain this phenomenon, geologists note the 'hot spot' theory. This suggests that in the region where Fernandina stands today there is a weakness in the earth's crust – a hot spot. Periodically, the build-up of pressure within the earth is released through this hot spot, manifested as a huge volcanic eruption. Over a period of several eruptions, the volcano becomes large enough to rise above sea level and form land. This new island then joins the others on the slow-moving 'conveyer belt'.

Charles Darwin and the theory of evolution

In 1835, the young Charles Darwin arrived on the Galápagos for a brief five-week visit. He landed only on San Cristóbal, Santiago, Floreana and Isabela, yet from his scant visit he deduced much about the geological formation of the islands and their biology. In particular, Darwin identified different species of finches living on different islands. In 1859 he published his revolutionary work *On the Origin of Species by Means of Natural Selection*. The entire edition sold out on its first day!

In it Darwin was able to provide evidence for plausible mechanisms which caused species to change, a process he called natural selection. Darwin realised that living species, from oak trees to turtles, produce more young than are intended to survive. Each species will show different requirements for survival, but, for example, a more cryptic colouration, or the ability to run faster, swim better or remain motionless, may give an individual an advantage over its siblings. This leads to it being selected naturally as a survivor.

At that time it was thought that species were divinely created, and never changed. Darwin proposed that over a long period of time, species gradually evolve. The changes were in response to their changing environment, by means of what he called natural selection. This was a mechanism by which those individuals that were better adapted were more likely to breed successfully. This same advantage may be inherited by its offspring. Gradually over time a new species may arise. So natural selection results in evolution.

Subsequent discoveries served only to strengthen Darwin's arguments. We now know that variation arises by mutations of the genetic code which may be passed on to succeeding generations. The key to speciation (the process by which new species arise) is isolation. Once populations are separated, mutations and natural selection will occur. Over time, if the populations diverge enough, they will no longer be able to interbreed, and hence new species will have formed. If a bird from the mainland establishes on an island it will diverge from the original population. As this process repeats itself, multiple related species evolve. This process, known as 'adaptive radiation', has occurred among several groups in the Galápagos: Darwin's finches, mockingbirds, lava lizards and among the daisy family.

The flightless cormorant (*Phalacrocorax harrisi*) possesses only tattered vestigial wings and cannot fly. As abundant food is available in nearby waters throughout the year, and there are no land predators, the bird no longer needs to fly, and smaller wings have proved more useful than larger ones. These also create less drag as the bird swims and allows the development of muscles appropriate for swimming. (JRG)

Having drifted away from the hot-spot area, an island experiences little or no more volcanic activity, and the now-dormant volcano is gradually eroded by wind and sea. In fact the term 'hot spot' has now been replaced by 'mantle plume', because the origin of the magma is thought to lie deep within the mantle.

The weight of the new volcano on the 'plastic' layer of molten rocks inside the earth causes the earth's crust to sag over time, which accelerates erosion. It is no surprise to find the southeasterly islands less dramatic in topography than those to the west. Española, the oldest island (between three and five million years old), is in fact so eroded that no evidence of a volcanic cone now exists. Apart from the normal agents of erosion such as wind and rain, volcanic islands also erode due to phenomena such as caldera collapses. In June 1968, the Fernandina caldera changed dramatically when its floor, a block 2km in diameter, fell by 350m over a nine-day period, in approximately 75 increments of about 5m each. The caldera was cloaked in choking dust, the lake water disappeared and many organisms died, including an estimated 2,000 white-cheeked pintail ducks and unknown numbers of land iguanas.

To the northwest of the archipelago is an extensive submarine rise known as the Carnegie Ridge. This is probably an extension of ex-Galápagos islands further along the conveyor belt which have long since eroded below sea level. Because of the ridge, the island group has been around a lot longer than Española, allowing the endemic fauna and flora to evolve into a unique compendium of species.

CLIMATE

The Galápagos are desert islands. There are two seasons – a warm, wet season which lasts from January to June, and a cool, dry season, known as the *garúa* season, from July to December. Seas are roughest during August and September. As altitude increases on the islands, air temperatures fall while precipitation increases.

Due to the isolated position of the archipelago, the climate is largely determined by ocean currents. In the cool season, the Humboldt Current flowing from the southeast keeps the islands cooler than their equatorial position would suggest. During this time a fine mist called *garúa* condenses in the air. This is formed by the temperature differences which occur at the place where cool, moist air hanging over the cold water meets a higher layer of air which is warmed by the hot sun. At this zone, called an inversion layer, mist cloaks the islands at a height of about 300–600m. Even in the warm, wet season there is very little rain in the coastal areas, except during an El Niño year, and the skies are blue with only occasional rainshowers. The action of the trade winds blowing from the southeast means the southwestern sides of the larger islands are the wettest. Average annual rainfall is about 229mm. Northwestern slopes of islands are in the rain shadow and are much drier at the sea surface, depending on locality and time of year. During a normal year, temperatures at sea level range between 15°C and 29°C.

El Niño – 'the Christchild'

The Galápagos Islands are regularly hit by the El Niño phenomenon, which leaves hundreds of sea lions, marine iguanas and seabird chicks dead in its wake. Every four to seven years, for reasons not yet fully understood, the southeast trade winds weaken or cease, causing ocean currents to slacken, which results in a massive shift in climatic conditions worldwide. This change generally begins around Christmas, hence the name (since 'El Niño' is Spanish for 'The Child' – the nickname for Christ). In most years, the westward-driving Pacific Ocean currents cause a stacking of water in the west Pacific, with sea levels half a metre higher than in the east. When currents slacken during an El Niño event, this warm water, which has been held at bay by the winds, slops back eastwards, bathing the Galápagos archipelago and beyond. Rain clouds form over warm seawater, hence the higher rainfall in the Galápagos and the western seaboard of South America.

The warm water is clear, lacking the nutrients normally found in the rich, cold, upwelling waters of the Humboldt Current. Many animals face starvation, while those that can leave do so. Fish such as sharks swim deeper to reach the cooler water beneath the warm surface layer. In the inter-tidal areas, new algae species grow which are unpalatable to the marine iguanas, so many of them die too. But the terrestrial environment booms. With vegetation triggered by the rains, finches, land iguanas and insects all do well.

Long-term prediction of an El Niño event is still not possible, although a network of buoys measures temperature, winds and currents in the tropical Pacific Ocean. These relay information via satellite to scientists, helping to predict at least short-term climate changes within the next six months. Also air-pressure differences between Darwin in Australia, and Tahiti give a reference figure known as the Southern Oscillation Index (SOI) which correlates to the intensity and duration of an El Niño event. The opposite of an El Niño, called a La Niña, is characterised by an accentuation of normal conditions, resulting in wetter wet seasons and drier dry seasons.

Facts about El Niño
- El Niño was first recognised by fishermen in the eastern Pacific as early as the late 1800s.
- El Niño effects are generally felt most strongly from December through May.
- In the Galápagos, marine-based organisms tend to suffer while terrestrial organisms experience bonanza years.
- As many as 50% of sea lions and marine iguanas die in the Galápagos during a large El Niño event. Many marine birds also die.
- Galápagos sea-surface temperatures soar to an average of 30°C or more during an El Niño event.
- Sea levels rise in the Galápagos and coastal Ecuador, causing loss of beaches and changing coastal habitats.
- Increased rainfall promotes tremendous plant growth, resulting in major habitat change.

Unlike many other species, land iguanas benefit from the increased vegetation following an El Niño event. (PO)

ISLAND HISTORY

The Galápagos Islands were officially discovered by Fray Tomás de Berlanga, the Bishop of Panama, in 1535, when his ship was becalmed in the Pacific and then swept off course. They appear to have been first named *Isolas de Galápagos* by a Flemish cartographer named Orteliu, in 1536. The name Galápagos originates from a Spanish word for saddle, or saddleback tortoise. The islands also became known as *Las Encantadas* (the Enchanted Isles), not for their beauty but for the menace of their strong currents, thick fog banks and small emergent rocks. By the late 1500s, pirates and buccaneers were regularly hiding out in the archipelago and by the 1680s, such famous buccaneers as William Dampier, Ambrose Cowley and Edward Davis, based in the Galápagos, were sacking the coastal towns of Ecuador and Peru.

Although the Galápagos originally appeared on a map in 1570, it was Cowley who first crudely charted the islands in 1684. In 1790, Alessandro Malaspina led the first scientific visit to the islands from Spain. This coincided with the arrival of the whalers. As industry grew in the developed world there was a rising demand for whale oil. In 1793, the whaler James Colnett arrived from Britain in HMS *Rattler*. Thus began the heyday of whaling, the period which certainly had the most biological impact on the islands. There were so many whales that Colnett reported seeing lines of them passing from dawn to dusk.

Post office barrel, Floreana Island (DH)

At about this time a post office barrel was established on Floreana Island, in which sailors would leave mail to be collected by ships that were homeward bound. In 1813, Captain David Porter was sent from the United States in the warship Essex to destroy the British whaling fleet, which he duly did. In 1905–6, an expedition from the California Academy of Sciences collected the skins of 6,000 land birds and 266 tortoises, among other prizes.

The first resident of the Galápagos was an unkempt and fearsome Irishman called Patrick Watkins who was marooned on Floreana in 1807 and stayed until 1809. In 1859, oil was discovered in the United States and the whaling industry declined. In 1832, the Galápagos Islands were annexed by Ecuador and colonised. Attempts were made to harvest dyer's moss, the lichen *Roccella babingtonii*, which was used as a dye in the textile industry. A small settlement established on Floreana quickly became a penal colony, and stories of subsequent tyranny, slavery and murder on the island abounded.

Charles Darwin (HB)

In 1835, a young scientist named Charles Darwin arrived as the naturalist on HMS *Beagle*, captained by Robert FitzRoy. FitzRoy mapped the coastline of the Galápagos with such accuracy that his charts were used by all ships until World War II; Darwin's findings inspired his thoughts on evolution, and later provided evidence for his theory of natural selection.

During the 20th century, settlers and scientists converged on the islands from all corners of the globe. In 1924, Norwegian immigrants landed on Floreana, then on Santa Cruz where they set up a fish-canning plant. Over the years the five islands were settled by various nations. Then, in 1959, the Government of Ecuador declared all areas without a human population to be a national park. In the same year, the Charles Darwin Foundation for the Galápagos Islands was set up in Brussels. This led directly to the establishment of the Charles Darwin Research Station on Santa Cruz (Ecuador), officially inaugurated in 1964. In 1968, the Ecuador government sent out the first two park wardens and so began the administration of the national park. Large-scale tourism started in 1970 with the arrival of a 58-passenger vessel. The Galápagos have never looked back. The human population has continued to swell and, with tourism, places increasing pressures on natural resources. Today, towns such as Puerto Ayora on Santa Cruz are busy little centres of commerce and trade, a far cry from the natural beauty beyond.

'Death in Eden'

In September 1929, the eccentric German philosopher Friedrich Ritter eloped to the Galápagos with his mistress Dore Strauch, having persuaded their respective spouses to live together. The pair had prudently removed all of their teeth and made a single set of stainless steel dentures to share between them. The Ritters set up their own personal Eden, where they were joined in August 1932 by Heinz and Margaret Wittmer and their son Harry. None of the Europeans really got along with the others, and the situation dramatically worsened when another German, the self-proclaimed Baroness von Wagner Bosquet, disembarked in October of the same year with her three lovers in tow. There followed a series of strange events culminating in several mysterious deaths and disappearances, which left Margaret Wittmer the sole survivor of the saga. She died in the year 2000 on Floreana at the age of 96.

Floreana (PO)

HABITATS

A Galápagos landscape of lava and ash (Bartolomé Island). (DH)

I solated islands are important distillations of life on earth. Only a select number of plants and animals manage to arrive, establish themselves and survive there. To compare wildlife in different places, scientists group collections of organisms into communities. A habitat is a geographical area where we may expect to find such a community, for example a seashore, a lava flow or a humid highland forest. Although in reality habitats all blend together, they are a useful concept. Larger islands such as Santa Cruz have a much greater range of habitats, so more species are found there.

The number of species found on an island also depends on its distance from other islands and from the mainland. The more isolated islands such as Española, Darwin and Genovesa have the fewest. However, those that do occur have become different from the same species on the central islands. For instance, on Española the marine iguanas are much more colourful, the mockingbirds have longer beaks, and the lizards are bigger than elsewhere.

Apart from plants that like salty conditions, it is the amount of moisture (or lack of it) that determines which plants can grow. This is related to underlying rock types, climate, ocean currents and altitude. The broad vegetation zones in the Galápagos can be described from coast to highlands. In general the higher you climb, the cooler and wetter it gets.

LITTORAL (COAST) ZONE

The littoral habitat is the narrow band along the coast. Mainly evergreen plants grow here, though their existence is due more to salt-tolerance than to climate. The four species of mangrove are the principal trees of the quiet lagoons. They are the red mangrove (*Rhizophora mangle*), the black mangrove (*Avicennia germinans*), the button mangrove (*Conocarpus erecta*) and the white mangrove (*Laguncularia racemosa*). The word mangrove is actually an ecological term rather than a scientific classification, since these four species come from different families of plant.

Pahoehoe lava flow (DH)

Erupting volcano, Fernandina Island (JRG)

Uplifted coral, Isabela Island (JR)

Typical arid zone scene with *Opuntia* cactus and land iguana
(*Conolophus subcristatus*) (South Plaza). (PO)

They do not compete, as each prefers slightly different growing conditions. The red mangrove grows with its roots in the sea (it is very important for stabilising mud), whereas black and white mangroves grow further away from the high-tide level. The other common plant is saltbush (*Cryptocarpus pyriformis*), which forms the backdrop to many beaches. Saltbush stores water in its fleshy leaves; these are quite salty if you chew them, hence the name. It provides shade for sea lions and nesting sites for pelicans and frigatebirds. All these plants have evolved internal desalination techniques more efficient than man-made ones.

On drier sand-dunes, smaller deep-rooted herbs like the seaside heliotrope (*Heliotropium curassavicum*), or succulents like sea purslane (*Sesuvium*), shrubs like clubleaf (*Nolana galapagensis*) and clinging vines like beach morning glory (*Ipomoea pes-caprae*), protect the sand and provide sustenance for land iguanas and insects. The common morning glory has long, pink, trumpet-shaped flowers. There is also an endemic white-flowered species, which prefers lava cliffs such as those on Genovesa. Shrubs such as mealy leaf (*Atriplex peruviana*), saltwort (*Batis maritima*) and leatherleaf (*Maytenus octogona*) exist where soil is present. A common plant found throughout the tropics is the inkberry or sea grape (*Scaevola plumieri*), whose black, round, fleshy fruits float in seawater.

The littoral zone is a habitat rich in invertebrates, molluscs, crustaceans and insects. Ghost crabs are a typical sight on the sands; fiddler crabs and oysters are seen in the mangrove lagoons. Marine iguanas live both in and out of the water, but nest ashore and only go to sea to feed on algae. Small fish such as gobies and blennies are found in the tide pools; in turn, they provide food for herons. In the muddy waters, brine shrimps provide both food and pigmentation for flamingos.

ARID ZONE

Beyond the reaches of salt spray is a broad zone of lava, ash and cinder where only plants able to exist with little moisture can survive. Here temperatures soar up to 30°C, especially during the hot season. Many of the plants lose their leaves during the cooler, drier season. It is an important zone, as a high proportion of endemic plants has evolved under these harsh conditions.

The shrubs and trees of the arid zone, nearly all of them unique to the archipelago, have adopted different strategies to cope with drought. Probably the most familiar is the prickly pear cactus (*Opuntia*) of which there are several species with large, yellow flowers and flat prickly pads. See box on page 26. The candelabra cactus (*Jasminocereus thouarsii*) is also treelike; the lava cactus (*Brachycereus nesioticus*) is a slow-growing herb which creates its own humus from dead cylindrical stems. It is a typical 'pioneer' plant that grows on barren lava flows. The only other herb to colonise recent volcanic rock is the tiny mollugo (*Mollugo flavescens*). This fragile endemic plant embodies Darwin's 'struggle for existence'. It manages to survive on overnight dew in cracks in the hard rock.

Scalesia forest, Santa Cruz Island (PO)

The evergreen chala (*Croton scouleri*) has very narrow leaves; the bitterbush (*Castela galapageia*) has small, waxy leaves. Other plants such as palo santo (*Bursera graveolens*) lose their leaves in the dry season. The acacias (*Leguminosae*) have spines. The leatherleaf (*Maytenus*) seen on the lower slopes has leaves that are vertical to receive less direct solar radiation. Almost all plants of the arid zone have deep or widespread roots, causing even spacing. An example is the grey matplant (*Tiquilia nesiotica*), which grows on the ash slopes of Bartolomé. See photo on page 7.

Few animals appear to live in this habitat. Reptiles such as land iguanas, lava lizards and snakes are quite at home, though even they avoid the midday sun by finding shade or burrowing into holes. Locusts, grasshoppers and other insects provide food for them. Spiders, scorpions and geckos can be found under rocks. Land birds such as finches, mockingbirds and warblers appear wherever a few patches of vegetation grow. Seabirds like blue-footed boobies actually like to raise their young on the flat, arid islands. They, too, have developed techniques for keeping cool, such as fluttering their gular throat skin to act as a ventilator.

The arid zone rises to about 200m. As elevation and humidity increase, larger trees appear. A transition zone between arid and humid has been recognised. Biodiversity increases here, and new deciduous trees such as pega-pega (*Pisonia floribunda*) or Galápagos guava (*Psidium galapageium*) replace the familiar palo santo. Lichens can be found throughout the arid zone, as they are tolerant to both dry and damp conditions.

HIGHLAND ZONE

The lush evergreen forest of the highlands surprises most visitors. The reason is the mist or *garúa* that the cool trade winds bring from the southeast. (These winds are strongest during the cool, 'dry' season.) The humid habitats are much wider on the southern or windward sides, and begin on average after 300m. From this height to about 700m is a zone dominated by a single tree, *Scalesia*, an endemic genus of the daisy or sunflower family. A visit to the highlands of Santa Cruz will take you right through this forest. *Scalesia* can reach 10m tall, but the majority of forest is made up of young trees 3–5m. This is because these trees have evolved to withstand drought, whereas during the high rainfall of an El Niño year the older ones rot away. On other islands like San Cristóbal, Santiago and Floreana, little native forest remains.

Higher up, trees such as cat's claw (*Zanthoxylum fagara*) and shrubs such as milkberry (*Chiococca alba*) appear, but the most distinctive change is the abundance of epiphytes. These are plants such as mosses, liverworts, bromeliads and vines that cling to others but are not parasites. The dense growth of brown mosses and liverworts has given the name 'brown zone' to the habitat above the *scalesia* forest. Few orchids have become established in the islands, because orchids rely on very specific pollinators who would have had to arrive at the same time. A native variety of guava (*Psidium galapageium*) provides hardwood,

Tortoise (*Geochelone elephantopus porteri*) cooling off in the Highland Zone (JRG)

and is rare for this reason. The introduced guava (*Psidium guayava*), on the other hand, has spread uncontrollably to become a pest; the worst area for this is southern Isabela.

On Santa Cruz and San Cristóbal another endemic shrub, *Miconia*, has given its name to the habitat above the *scalesia* and 'brown' zones. Few tall trees grow but liverworts, lichens and mosses abound. Sadly the pinkish-flowered *miconia* has been almost wiped out by human activity and fires. It needs protection as much as the animals of Galápagos.

Above the *miconia* habitat there are few trees. The tallest species is the tree fern *Cyathea weatherbyana*, which can reach 3m. Mostly the eroded uplands are covered in ferns, grasses and sedges. This habitat is known locally as the Pampa, which means grassland. Few plants here are native to the islands; they are mostly long-distance travellers like sphagnum moss or club moss (*Lycopodium*). Their tiny spores can be carried into the upper

Miconia (DH)

atmosphere and be distributed for thousands of miles. The introduction of the quinine plant cinchona, or cascarilla, has also had a detrimental effect on all the highland habitats. It is a native of the high Andes.

Lava cactus (*Brachycereus nesiolicus*) (JRG)

Though it is the animals of the Galápagos that have caught the world's eye, the flora is just as interesting to the naturalist. The absence of gymnosperms (conifers, etc), the small number of monocotyledons (lilies, palms) and the abundance of 'weedy' asters of the daisy family are telling. This uneven range of families supports the geologists' view that the islands were never connected to the mainland. The ocean has acted as a 'filter' in allowing a select few families to arrive. The majority of plants would have arrived on the wind or attached to birds' feet or feathers.

The first to colonise would probably have been lichens, which can grow on rocks without soil. Later arrivals include ferns and asters, which are easily dispersed (think of a dandelion's seeds). Over 700 'higher' species (flowering plants and ferns) have been recognised so far, with approximately two-thirds native and one-third introduced by humans. Of the natives, a high proportion (40%) are endemic, with the rest also found in other places. Of these, nearly all arrived from South America, with the odd Central American species.

The accidentally and deliberately introduced plants have had a catastrophic effect on native vegetation. For example, elephant grass sown on Santa Cruz for pasture has spread along the road within decades, replacing unique plants which evolved on the volcano slopes. Most non-native species were introduced for agricultural purposes or forestry; others were introduced as ornaments or by accident.

PLANTS OF THE LITTORAL ZONE

Herbs (non-woody)

- **Beach morning glory** (*Ipomoea pes-caprae*, Convolvulacae) A long, creeping vine with stout stems, common on sand dunes. Long, trumpet-shaped purple flowers. An endemic species with white flowers (*Ipomoea habeliana*) is found on lava, and another with pink flowers on ashy material.
- **Milkwort** (*Polygala spp*, Polygalaceae) Slender red-stemmed herb. Small, white flowers with yellow centres. Grows on dry, sandy soil.
- **Sea purslane** (*Sesuvium spp*, Aizoaceae) These salt-tolerant herbs have succulent leaves that store moisture. They are bright green during the hot season, after the rains, but turn red in the dry season (this is thought to be a way of slowing down metabolism

Top Milkwort (*Polygala spp*) (DH)
Above Seaside heliotrope or scorpion weed (*Heliotropium curassavicum*) (DH)

16

during the drought). Form reddish mats on South Plaza Island. *S. portulacastrum* has tiny pinkish star-shaped flowers, while the endemic *S. edmonstonei* has white flowers. See photo on page 19.

- **Seaside heliotrope or Scorpion weed** (*Heliotropium curassavicum*, Boraginaceae) A low-growing tiny herb with slightly hairy stem. The curved inflorescence is distinctive with small white flowers on one side. Long bluish-grey leaves. Common on sand dunes.
- **Sedges** (Cyperaceae) Have flowers in whorls at top of stems. Resemble grass but distinguished by triangular stems. Grow on lava and coastal sands.
- **Shore petunia** (*Exodeconus miersii*, Solanaceae) Large shield-shaped leaves, hairy stems, and white trumpet-shaped flowers form mats on the ground.

Sedge (*Cyperus andersonii*) (DH)

Galápagos cotton (*Gossypium darwinii*) (DH)

Shore petunia (*Exodeconus miersii*) (DH)

Red mangrove seed (*Rhizophora mangle*) (PO)   Galápagos lantana (*Lantana peduncularis*) (DH)

Shrubs

- **Clubleaf** (*Nolana galapagoensis*) Dense shrub with distinctive club-shaped, fleshy leaves in clusters. The white flowers are fused into a tube, but rarely seen. Common on the dunes of Punta Cormorant's south beach.
- **Leatherleaf** (*Maytenus octogona*) Tiny green flowers not very distinctive, but hard, waxy leaves characteristic in their vertical orientation. Fruit capsules open to reveal red berries.
- **Mealy leaf** (salt sage, *Atriplex peruviana*, Chenopodiaceae) Small shrub or herb with pale wrinkled leaves. Small browny-yellow flowers at ends of branches. Salt tolerant. Common at Punta Suárez on Española.

Clubleaf (*Nolana galapagoensis*) (DH)   Leatherleaf (*Maytenus octogona*) (DH)

- **Saltbush** (*Cryptocarpus pyriformis*, Nyctaginacea) A common fringe to most beaches. Forms dense bushes, green all year. Large, irregular, fleshy leaves. Small green flowers at the ends of branches have five fused sepals with no petals.

Mealy leaf (*Atriplex peruviana*) (DH)

Saltbush (*Cryptocarpus pyriformis*) (DH)

White mangrove (*Laguncularia racemosa*) (DH)

Button mangrove (*Conocarpus erecta*) (PO)

Trees
- **Red mangrove** (*Rhizophora mangle*) Commonest of the four mangroves, has prop roots that grow in muddy water or on rocks in the inter-tidal zone. These filter out salt so almost pure water reaches the rest of the plant. Leaves thick and waxy. The characteristic long fruit dangle over the water, then drop and float away to grow elsewhere. Important in stabilising coasts. Can grow to 7m.

Black mangrove (*Avicenna germinans*) (DH)

- **White mangrove** (*Laguncularia racemosa*) Small oval leaves, paler than other species. On the underside the leaves have pores near the edges which are for excreting salt. Though salt-tolerant they grow slightly above the inter-tidal zone, and can reach 8m. Flowers are tiny, white and in clusters.
- **Black mangrove** (*Avicennia germinans*) Leaves long, pointed, dark green above, lighter grey below. Small white clusters of flowers and oval, hairy, yellowish fruits. Common in brackish lagoons, they have roots called 'pneumatophores' that project vertically from the mud. Fruits also float. The largest mangrove; can reach 20m.
- **Button mangrove** (*Conocarpus erecta*) This shrub or tree grows 2–10m tall. Small oval leaves which are hairy underneath, as are the stems. Greenish flowers in dense, round clusters at the ends of branches (no petals); fruits are also small and round, but brown like cones.

PLANTS OF THE ARID ZONE
Herbs

- **Mollugo** (*Mollugo flavescens*) Tiny endemic herb, a pioneer on lava. Tan-coloured stems. Leaves narrow to oval. Small, whitish flowers. This rare plant has evolved species ende micto particular lava flows, such as *Mollugo crockeri* found at Sullivan Bay.

Mollugo (*Mollugo sp*) (DH)

Grey matplant (*Tiquilia resiotica*) (DH)

Passion flower (*Passiflora foetida*) (DH)

- **Galápagos tomato** (*Solanum cheesmaniae*, Solanaceae) An endemic tomato; a low, branching, hairy herb. Spear-shaped leaves. Darwin observed seeds germinate better after passing through the gut of a tortoise. Small, edible fruits whose DNA has been used to breed salt- and drought-resistant tomatoes.
- **Grey matplant** (*Tiquilia nesiotica*, Boraginaceae) This endemic herb has a woody base, grey all over. Tiny white flowers are hidden among the leaves. It colonises ash slopes on Bartolomé.
- **Passion flower** (*Passiflora foetida*, Passifloraceae) This endemic subspecies of vine has long, trailing, hairy stems, and broad, three-pointed leaves. Flowers are large and white, hairy and green below, and have a purple centre with vertical reproductive parts. Feathery bracts, green or yellow when ripe, protect the fruits.

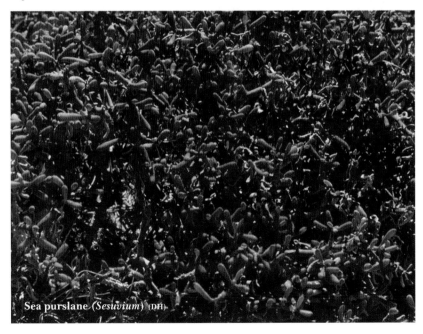

Sea purslane (*Sesuvium*) (DH)

- **Puncture vine** (goat's head, *Tribulus cistoides*) The bane of the barefoot guide, this ground-dwelling, hairy herb has composite leaves and yellow flowers on stalks. Fruits have two sharp spines that can penetrate the toughest sole. The large ground finch is the only creature that finds the fruit attractive. See photo on page 21.
- **Purslane** (*Portulaca oleracea*) At first resembles sea purslane, a similar succulent-leafed herb, but distinguished by larger yellow flowers. A favoured food of the land iguanas on South Plaza.
- **Spurge** (*Chamaesyce amplexicaulis*, Euphorbiaceae) Woody at the base, with a milky sap, opposing leaves and tiny white flowers. Grows on lava or ash near the sea. Noticeable at start of summit trail on Bartolomé. Several species, each with very different leaves.

Shrubs and trees
- **Acacia** (*Leguminosae mimosaceae*) A drought resistant tree with sharp spines, composite leaves, flowers in small orange balls, and fruits in dry long pods.
- **Bitterbush/Amargo** (*Castela galapageia*) Dense shrub with spines. Small, dark, oval leaves, shiny on top. Flowers red outside, yellow inside, grow at base of leaves. Distinctive fruits like red berries. Common at James Bay, South Plaza and Punta Cormorant.
- **Cacti** See box on page 26.

Top left Purslane (*Portulaca oleracea*) (DH), *Top right* Spurge (*Chamaesyce amplexicaulis*) (DH)
Above left Acacia (*Acacia macracantha*) (DH), *Above right* Bitterbush (*Castela galapageia*) (DH)

Top left Cutleaf daisy (*Lecocarpus pinnatifidus*) (DH), *Top right* Palo santo (*Bursera graveolens*) (DH)
Above Daisy trees (*Scalesia Spp*) at the Los Gemelos craters on Santa Cruz (PO)

- **Cutleaf daisy** (*Lecocarpus pinnatifidus*, Asteraceae) This has very irregular fleshy and hairy leaves, with composite, yellow, daisy-like flowers on a stalk. Only found on Floreana, especially near the coast.
- **Darwin's daisy** (*Darwiniothamnus tenuifolius*) Many-branching, small shrub with long, hairy, narrow leaves and compact flower heads at ends of branches. See photo on page 25.
- **Daisy tree** (lechoso, *Scalesia spp*) Though this composite genus dominates the humid forests, other species are found in the dry zone. Fifteen species occur throughout the archipelago and, like the finches, probably evolved from a single ancestor species. Each has a composite white head of flowers and hairy leaves; for example, *Scalesia villosa* on Floreana. See photo on page 12.
- **Galápagos cotton** (*Gossypium darwinii*) Large endemic shrub, black dots on stems, leaves three-lobed, large flowers, yellow petals with reddish-purple base. Fruits are dry capsules that open to reveal white lint inside. Finches use this for nesting material. See photo on page 17.

- **Galápagos lantana** (*Lantana peduncularis*, Verbenaceae) Small, thin, angular twigged shrub. Leaves have a toothed edge, disappear during the dry season. Small, white flowers with fused petals in five lobes, one of which is larger. A coloured introduced species is in danger of spreading where the native species grows.

Manzanillo (*Hippomane mancinella*) and palo santo (*Bursera graveolens*) trees growing on a cool lava field, Santiago (PO)

- **Manzanillo/poison apple** (*Hippomane mancinella*, Euphorbiaceae) A tree with thick, oval leaves, whose fruit resembles a small apple. The whole tree including the fruit is poisonous; just touching the bark can cause irritation.
- **Palo santo** (*Bursera graveolens*) The Spanish name translates as 'holy-stick' for two reasons: it flowers at Christmas, and its incense-like resin is used in churches on the mainland. The tree rapidly turns green in the rainy season. For most of the year it is leafless and grey, with lichen-covered bark.
- **Thorn shrub** (espino, *Scutea pauciflora*) A mass of green spines with almost invisible flowers and few leaves.
- **Velvet shrub** (*Waltheria ovata*) Small shrub with distinctive dark bark, serrated leaves with veins. Small, yellow flowers.

PLANTS OF THE HIGHLAND ZONE

Space does not permit us to describe all the plants of this region. We have described some of the principal plants such as *scalesia*, *miconia*, and ferns, grasses and sedges above (see *Highland* section). Lichens are common here too, including epiphytic species, which grow on other plants instead of rocks. Other epiphytes like bromeliads and mosses are common in the 'brown zone'. Another primitive plant, related to ferns, is *Lycopodium spp*, confusingly named 'club-moss'. These plants look like miniature Christmas trees.

Top left Velvet shrub (*Waltheria ovata*) (DH)
Left Club-moss (*Lycopodium cernuum*) (DH)

Highland epiphytes (DH)

Below left Galápagos tomato
(*Solanum cheesmaniae*) (DH)
Bottom left Puncture vine
(*Tribulus cistoides*) (DH)

Below right Darwin's daisy
(*Darwiniothamnus tenuifolius*) (DH)
Bottom right Beach morning glory
(*Ipomoea pes-caprae*) (DH)

Galápagos cacti

Cacti are able to store water in their spongy pads and can survive long periods of drought. The thin spines are thought to have evolved from leaves, and their pads from stems. All the species are endemic.

- **Candelabra cactus** (*Jasminocereus thouarsii*) A tall cactus with ribbed branches that reach upwards to 7m. Flowers are green or purple and open before dawn, probably pollinated by moths. The fruits are purple and edible when ripe.
- **Lava cactus** (*Brachycereus nesioticus*) Has short finger-like clumps of brownish, cylindrical branches. Many spines of variable lengths, yellow in colour, darkening when mature. A 'pioneer' plant which grows on young lava flows. Flowers have large white petals, also open pre-dawn. See photo on page 15.
- **Prickly pear** (*Opuntia spp*, known as *tuna* in Spanish) Though found throughout the new world, species here have evolved into unique forms (14 subspecies). On some islands, eg: North Seymour, a shrublike version exists; on others, eg: Santa Cruz, a giant tree variety has evolved, which can grow to 12m tall. Another species on Santa Fé has a huge girth, over 1m in diameter. The traditional explanation is that browsing by tortoises has caused the gigantism, but other factors such as competition for light have also played a part. Land iguanas feed on the pads, flowers and fruits. The northern island's subspecies have soft spines that could encourage land birds to pollinate them where pollinating insects are absent.

Opuntia flowers are bright yellow and a favourite food of the cactus finch and dove, but the carpenter bee is thought to be the chief pollinator The large fruits are green to red and shaped like a child's spinning top. Land iguanas roll them to remove the spines prior to devouring them. The pads provide food for tortoises who seem oblivious to the spines. They are also a source of moisture for birds, reptiles and even the endemic rice rat.

The giant species have a reddish bark. which flakes off in translucent scales. Galápagos *opuntias* close their pores during the heat of the day and open them at night to reduce water loss. They do not have deep roots and may become top-heavy; the severe rains and winds of an El Niño can topple them.

A giant prickly pear cactus (*Opuntia spp*) on Santa Fé island (PO)

INVERTEBRATES

Silver fritillary (*Agraulis vanillae galapagoensis*) (DH)

Top left Centipede
(*Scolopendra galapagoensis*) (DH)
Above left Scorpion
(*Hadruroides maculatus galapagoensis*) (DH)

Top right Polistes versicolor (PO)
Above right Painted locust
(*Schistocerca melanocera*) (PO)

The Galápagos Islands are certainly not known for their land invertebrates, yet many such as the tiny *Bulimulid* snails are incredible examples of speciation – far more varied than Darwin's finches. There are at least 65 snail species reported in the islands, all of them endemic. They are very inconspicuous, living in damp areas in lava crevices and under leaves.

Stewart Peck, a researcher from Carleton University, has gone a long way to quantifying the Galápagos land and freshwater invertebrates. The current count, continuously rising, is a total of 2,257 species, 51% of which are endemic. Terrestrial invertebrates include 83 land snails, 114 spiders, approximately 400 mites, 24 other arachnids (ticks and spider relatives), 12 centipedes and millipedes, and 1,530 insects. These numbers, however, are very low when compared with those of similar habitats on the mainland. Of the very limited number of these invertebrates which will be seen by the visitor to the islands, few are particularly exciting.

The largest group by far is the arthropods (this name means jointed limbs). It includes insects, scorpions, centipedes, spiders and ticks. All arthropods have a tough outer shell (the exoskeleton) which they must moult in order to grow. They are extremely varied in shape and behaviour. Only very few, the more conspicuous species, will be dealt with here.

INSECTS
Ants, bees, wasps and beetles

Of the *Hymenoptera* (ants, bees and wasps), the carpenter bee *Xylocopa darwinii* is the most prominent. Large, conspicuous, solitary bees, male carpenters are reddish-brown and relatively rare, while the more common females are black. One of the most important pollinators of the islands, their name derives from their habit of making a neat hole in wood in which to nest. Two recent introductions to the islands are a wasp, *Polistes versicolor*, and the little fire ant *Wasmannia auropunctata*. Both have become serious pests. The more aggressive wasp *Brachygastra lecheguana* was accidentally introduced only in February 1994.

There are over 400 beetle species in the islands. One

Female carpenter bee (*Xylocopa darwinii*) (PO)

important species is *Trox suberosus*, a scarab beetle, the larvae of which attack the eggs of Pacific green turtles and can destroy whole clutches.

Butterflies and moths

Most conspicuous of the insects are the butterflies (at least eight species) and moths (over 350 species). Common butterflies include the large-tailed skipper *Urbanus dorantes*, a brown butterfly with swallow-tail-shaped hind wings. A fast flier, it is common in the highlands. At rest it sits with its wings held slightly open. The endemic Galápagos blue butterfly (*Leptotes parrhasioides*) is rather small but very attractive on close examination. It belongs to the widely distributed family of 'blue butterflies', and is typical of them, flying low to the ground with a fast wingbeat. The Galápagos sulphur butterfly *Phoebis sennae marcellina* is a subspecies endemic to the islands where it is common and very conspicuous, being the only yellow butterfly present. The Galápagos silver fritillary *Agraulis vanillae galapagoensis* (see photo page 27) is another endemic subspecies common in most habitats. Its wings are black and orange with silver spots on the undersides. Other butterflies include two species of painted ladies, *Vanessa carye* and *Vanessa virginensis*, the well-known monarch butterfly *Danaus plexippus* of North America, and the related queen butterfly, *Danaus gilippus*.

The most conspicuous moths are the various species of hawkmoths (Sphingidae): heavy-bodied, with a powerful flight and wingbeats so rapid they

Top Large-tailed skipper butterfly (*Urbanus dorantes*) (DH)
Above Galápagos blue butterfly (*Leptotes parrhasioides*) (DH)

Queen butterfly (*Danaus gilippus*) (DH)

appear as a blur. Mostly nocturnal, they are also sometimes seen by day hovering by flowers with their long proboscis (tongue), nearly twice their body length, probing the depths and sipping the nectar. They are sometimes mistaken for hummingbirds which they superficially resemble when flying.

Orthopterans

Of the *Orthopterans*, the insect order which includes grasshoppers, locusts and crickets, the endemic painted locust *Schistocerca melanocera* is the Galápagos Islands' largest insect, reaching up to about 8cm in length, with black, green, red and yellow colouring. It is very common, particularly in the lowland areas. You may spot one being eaten by a lava lizard, particularly at Puerto Egas on Santiago Island.

Silver fritillary butterfly (*Agraulis vanillae galapagoensis*) (DH)

SPIDERS

There are a few noteworthy species of spider. The crab spiders belong to the Thomisidae family and *Heteropoda venatoria* to the Sparassidae family. *Heteropoda venatoria* are often seen in hotel rooms on the islands, and occasionally on boats. They are harmless hunters and should be welcomed as expert pest controllers. A more sinister relative is the endemic *Latrodectus apicalis*, a small, round-bodied spider which lives under bark, rocks and logs. It is a relative of the black widow spider, and its bite may be dangerous. This spider is not commonly found.

The silver argiope spider, *Argiope argentata*, is a distinctive web-building spider. It has a silvery body and sits in the centre of its web at the hub of a bright silver, silky cross, its legs held together in pairs so they look like four legs following the lines of the cross.

Spider (*Neoscona oaxacensis*) (PO)

Another web-builder is *Neoscona oaxacensis*, which is also a relatively heavy-bodied spider. Its webs often span the narrow island trails, while the spider itself sits in wait under a leaf at the edge.

The beautiful star spider, *Gasteracantha cancriformis*, is also noteworthy. Living mostly in the coastal areas, this spider has an abdomen protected by heavy spines, while the body is a brilliant, glossy yellow and black.

SCORPIONS

There are two scorpion species. One, the endemic *Centruroides exsul*, is found only on Española, San Cristóbal, Santa Cruz and Pinta (an unusual distribution). The other, *Hadruroides maculatus galapagoensis*, occurs on most of the major islands. See photo page 28. Neither has a particularly serious sting, although it may well be painful. Scorpions, often found in houses in the towns, are active nocturnal hunters that feed on most other arthropods. They first capture victims in their heavy claws, then sting them to death by injecting poison from their flexible tails.

CENTIPEDES

Despite the presence of large hammerhead sharks, Galápagos sharks, and bull sea lions, probably the most feared animal in the archipelago is an invertebrate – the impressive endemic centipede, *Scolopendra galapagoensis* (see photo page 28). It grows to 30cm in length and its head is armed with a large pair of envenomating jaws capable of delivering a very painful, poisonous bite. Birds, such as hawks, which feed on it seem unaffected by the venom. When disturbed, it moves quickly over the ground in snake-like fashion to disappear under cover. A very agile, active predator, it feeds mainly on various arthropods, but will also kill lava lizards and even young birds. It is hardly seen except by residents whose houses it shares.

REPTILES

Giant tortoises (*Geochelone elephantopus*) (DH)

Dome-shaped tortoise (*Geochelone elephantopus vandenburghi*) on Volcán Alcedo, Isabela (JRG)

The Galápagos Islands are a veritable reptile haven. Having a dry, waterproof skin and good drought-resisting capabilities, reptiles can relatively easily negotiate long ocean crossings with no fresh water, to arrive and establish themselves on islands. The Galápagos are one of the world's rare ecosystems in which the top natural herbivores are reptiles: giant tortoises, land iguanas and even the coastal marine iguana.

The equatorial setting of the islands is ideally suited to reptiles, which rely on external heat sources to function. Unlike mammals, which control their body temperature by complex physiological means, reptiles must first warm up using the sun's energy, and then control their body temperature by adopting thermoregulatory behaviour – if they get too hot, they move into the shade or water; too cool, and they move back into the sun. At night they become sluggish. They also fine-tune body temperature by altering their posture, to present a greater or lesser surface area to the sun. In iguanas and lizards, temperature is also regulated using the pineal body, 'the third eye' in the brain, which may open through a transparent scale on top of the head. This acts as a light receptor, telling the animal when it has received enough solar radiation and should change posture. (The transparent scale can easily be seen by close inspection of a marine or land iguana.) Contrary to the popular belief that reptiles are cold-blooded, they may actually function at optimum temperatures greater than our own!

There are 23 species of reptile in Galápagos, plus some marine visitors and introduced species. All but two are endemic to the archipelago, with some endemic to specific islands. Many species such as the giant tortoises are on their way to evolving into new species but, at present, evolutionarily speaking, are still only at subspecies level, and could easily cross-breed if the different subspecies came into contact with each other.

TORTOISES

GIANT TORTOISE (*Geochelone elephantopus*)
To think of Galápagos is to think of tortoises. Indeed, the very name Galápagos is derived from an old Spanish word referring to their saddle-like shape. They are undoubtedly the archipelago's most celebrated animals, and it is a shame that their story is a sad one. They have suffered badly at the hands of humans and many races would no longer be around but for recent intervention.

The only other place in the world with any giant tortoises left still is the island of Aldabra in the Indian Ocean which, due to its remoteness, has remained virtually unaltered. While the Galápagos today have an estimated 15,000–17,000, Aldabra has a community almost ten times greater, living on a single atoll with a land area substantially less than Floreana. Although the Galápagos probably never had such a high density it must have been incredible to see the tortoises in their heyday. Today, the best places to see wild tortoises in the Galápagos are the highlands of Santa Cruz or Volcán

Today there are only 11 Galápagos tortoise subspecies surviving, one of which, *Geochelone elephantopus abingdoni* from Pinta, is represented by a single individual now living in captivity, fondly named 'Lonesome George' (shown here). (DH)

Alcedo on Isabela, although Alcedo is temporarily closed at present while the park wardens eradicate feral goats on the volcano.

Once there were very likely over 200,000 animals distributed throughout the archipelago, separated geographically into probably 14 subspecies. The islands on which tortoises have become extinct since the arrival of man are Floreana, Santa Fé, Fernandina and Rábida. The last two islands, however, have only ever produced a single specimen each. The subspecies claimed for Rábida, in particular, is dubious.

In the days of sail, long before refrigeration, sailors had a diet of weevil-ridden biscuits and salted pork. Any fresh meat was welcome. Between the late 1500s and the 1800s, two major events dramatically affected the future of the tortoise populations in Galápagos. First, as many as 100,000 were collected for food. Tortoises are well known for their resistance to drought and very slow metabolisms, and it was discovered that they would remain alive, upside-down in the holds of vessels, for up to a year with no food or water. Sailors were delighted with their dependable, rather tasty, fresh protein. Fats of the tortoises can be metabolised to produce water which keeps them alive (100g of fat will produce 107g of water). Unfortunately, mostly females were collected, as they were found closer to shore, and were smaller and more manageable. This greatly distorted the sex ratios and potential recovery speed of the population. In 1831–68 alone, 67 boats took 10,000 tortoises in 151 visits.

Secondly, pirates, whalers, sealers, buccaneers and colonists all introduced various mammals to the islands as an alternative food to be hunted on future visits. Goats, pigs, donkeys, dogs and rats (accidentally introduced) now prove a far greater and more insoluble problem: competing for grazing, damaging nests, eating eggs and young, and changing forest to grassland.

In the wild, a Galápagos tortoise may weigh up to a remarkable 270kg, with a curved carapace length of 1.22m. (A captive individual in Florida has attained a massive 385.1kg and is still growing!) With great size comes longevity. Unsubstantiated stories abound of tortoises more than 200 years old, but probably the most reliable record of age is an Aldabran subspecies (a relative of the Galápagos tortoise) which eventually died of an accident having reached at least 152 years. There are no confirmed records of great age among Galápagos tortoises, although they probably live for well over 100 years.

Today most tortoises in Galápagos live on Isabela, where each of the five main volcanoes has a relatively stable subspecies. Volcán Alcedo hosts over half the island's entire tortoise population. The other large colony is on Santa Cruz, with other, smaller, populations on San Cristóbal, Santiago and Pinzón. 'Lonesome George', long thought to be the only survivor of the failing 11th subspecies, may not be the last of his kind: back in 1981, a tortoise dropping was discovered on Pinta, his native island. However, another tortoise was never found. There is a long-standing reward of $10,000 for anyone able to produce a Pinta female, but by now most avenues of investigation have been exhausted. At present, George is housed with some similar tortoises from Volcán Wolf, in the hope that any offspring produced could eventually be back-crossed by scientists to approximate a new Pinta strain.

Two extreme types of carapace (the domed part of the tortoise's shell) have evolved in the Galápagos. They are so varied in shape, with so many intermediate forms, that Darwin was told, rather exaggeratedly, by the vice-governor of the islands at the time of his visit, that he knew which island a tortoise came from by its carapace. Although there is truth in this claim, there is actually a great deal of overlap between many populations.

The two extreme types of shell shape do nevertheless represent tortoises from different habitats. The first form, the 'saddleback', is found in very arid habitats, and is smaller than the second – the dome-shaped carapace. Saddleback tortoises, such as those on Española and Pinzón, are much more aggressive amongst themselves than dome-shaped tortoises, because their main resources are limited, particularly food plants, water and shade. In a tortoise dominance contest, two rivals approach each other and stretch their front legs, head and neck as high as they can, with mouth agape. The tallest tortoise wins. There is very little, if any, actual fighting as with some tortoise species. The tallest animals can reach furthest, so extra height brings the added advantage of more food. This reinforces the transfer of 'height' genes from one generation to the next.

The front end of a saddleback tortoise's shell is raised, exposing a lot of soft skin. In their dry habitat, however, there is no dense ground cover of vegetation which could injure the animal when it is on the move; and with no native predators, the lesser protection inherent in the saddleback was of no consequence during evolution.

Dome-shaped tortoises, much more typical of the rest of the world's tortoise species, are found in moister areas with plenty of lush vegetation, water and shade, so have not needed to become antagonistic and evolve an extra height advantage for dominance. Also, when they are negotiating the

Saddleback tortoise
(*Geochelone elephantopus hoodensis*) (PO)

dense undergrowth of vegetation, the closed front end of the carapace gives them a useful tank-like quality.

Breeding strategies differ. Dome-shaped females dig two to three nests a year with up to 20 eggs per nest. In a harsher environment, saddlebacks dig four to five nests a year with an average of six eggs per clutch, in order to spread the risk.

In dome-shaped tortoises, males are about double the weight of females. Males stay in the highlands, while the females tend to migrate towards the coast when ready to lay their eggs to find temperatures better suited

Tortoise highway! Galápagos tortoises (*Geochelone elephantopus*) use regular, well-worn paths for ease of travel across difficult terrain. (JRG)

to incubation. Most eggs are laid between June and December. The female digs the nest laboriously with her hind feet, so she cannot see what she is doing. Eventually, after many hours, she manages to create a neat cylindrical chamber, using her strong claws and copious urine to bind the soil, and drops her tennis-ball-sized eggs inside. These are left to the sun to incubate, and, apart from a final urination on the filled-in nest (which hardens to form a toughened cap), she has no further involvement and ambles away. Incubation takes 160–240 days.

It is interesting that many reptiles have no sex gene, and the sex of the offspring is determined by the temperature of incubation during a critical stage of development. Warmer nests tend to result in females, cooler nests in males. Nests of a middling temperature may give a mixture of male and female hatchlings. The temperature of incubation is determined by the position of the nest: in shade, lower down the slope, etc. Another negative spin-off of sailors having collected mostly females on the lower slopes in pirate days was that these females also happened to be genetically programmed to lay nests in warmer areas, thus producing mostly female hatchlings. As we see, any interference with nature by man may have more far-reaching implications than first meet the eye. However, temperature-dependent sex determination is a useful laboratory tool whereby scientists, aiming at repatriating artificially-reared tortoises to the wild, can manipulate incubation temperatures to produce more females than males where necessary.

Having emerged from their leathery eggshells between December and April, the hatchlings struggle to break out of the nest. Their only natural predator is the Galápagos hawk, as Darwin observed in 1845: 'The young tortoises, as soon as they are hatched, fall prey in great numbers to the carrion-feeding buzzard.' Nowadays introduced rats also represent a major threat to hatchlings until they reach several years old and become 'rat proof'.

Tortoises reach sexual maturity between 20 and 25 years of age. In order to mate, the male tortoise climbs on to the female's back and reaches under her shell with his long tail, which houses his penis. His plastron (the underpart of the shell) is highly convex so that her carapace fits snugly into the depression and he does not roll off. Mating is a very lengthy and noisy process, and the loud, rhythmic grunts of the male can be heard 100m away or more. When hormonal levels are running high, male tortoises have even been known to try mounting rounded rocks resembling females. The only other sound that a tortoise makes is a loud hiss when frightened, caused by a sudden retraction of head and limbs into the shell, which rapidly expels air from the lungs via the nostrils. A tortoise's ribs cannot be expanded as they are fused to the carapace. To breathe, the tortoise has special muscles which create a negative pressure in the body and draw air in. Other muscles work to exhale spent air.

Tortoises are vegetarians and are known to feed on well over 50 plant species in the Galápagos. The *Opuntia* cacti are particularly significant in the drier areas, where they may also provide important sources of water.

During the breeding period many 'amphibious landing craft' tracks can be seen on sandy beaches, leading to and from the water. These are the tracks of the nesting female Pacific green turtles (*Chelonia mydas agassisi*). (JRG)

TURTLES

PACIFIC GREEN TURTLE (*Chelonia mydas agassisi*)
The Galápagos is one of the few areas of the world where turtles are still a common sight. Although hawksbill, olive ridley and leatherback turtles are all known from the Galápagos, the Pacific green turtle is by far the most common, and is the only species which nests in the islands. Green turtles are large, reaching over 150kg in weight, with a carapace length up to 1.3m. Adults have a primarily vegetarian diet, whereas the young eat virtually everything.

Green turtles breed at any time of the year, but most concentratedly in the hotter months. The female comes ashore under cover of darkness, and laboriously works her way up above the high-tide mark. Here she digs a shallow body pit by flicking huge quantities of sand backwards with her front flippers. When it is deep enough, she dexterously digs a cylindrical hole using her rear flippers, which form perfect scoops. Once the hole is complete, she lays a clutch of 70–100 eggs the size and shape of ping-pong balls. She heads back to the sea before the hot sun catches her high, dry and vulnerable, only to return perhaps once or twice more in the season to repeat the whole process. As with the giant tortoises (see page 35), warm nests give rise to female turtles and cooler ones result in males. During the breeding period males will try to mount anything; one even tried to climb on to me while I was snorkelling!

A young green turtle hatchling (*Chelonia mydas agassisi*) (PO)

41

Male Pacific green turtles (*Chelonia mydas agassisi*) hang around close to shore and mate repeatedly with as many females as possible. The male is smaller than the female and clings on to her shell using small hooks on the leading edges of his front flippers. (DH)

Apart from the total loss of turtle eggs on any beaches where the omniverous feral pigs (with truffle-hunting noses) are present, there is a natural enemy, the Trox beetle. These little insects burrow into the clutch and feed on the eggs.

After 45–55 days of incubation, the surviving turtles hatch from their leathery eggs and 'swim' upwards through the sand. Turtles are programmed to produce as many eggs as possible, since the vast majority will not survive to maturity (in the green turtle, 25–50 years). Evolutionarily speaking, the idea is to produce more young than predators can eat, thereby ensuring at least some offspring to launch the next generation. Eventually, through natural selection, only the fittest animals will survive.

The key element, however, is timing; the hatchling turtles must erupt *en masse* in order for some to escape the predators. Within the nest, the eggs in the middle of the clutch are warmer than those on the outside, due to the metabolic heat produced during development. The warmer the eggs, the faster they develop, which should put them out of synch with the outer eggs. Yet scientific experiment has shown that the wriggling stimulus of the better developed embryos actually accelerates the growth of the others, so that they catch up and all burst out together. The young turtles need to hatch at night on a high tide to have a good chance of reaching the sea. They run a harrowing gauntlet past marauding frigatebirds, pelicans, mockingbirds, hawks, ghost crabs, herons and more. Even on reaching the water they are not safe, since frigates take them from above while patrolling sharks snatch them from below. Once at sea, they swim continuously for days to escape the great risk of predation inshore.

LIZARDS AND SNAKES

LAND IGUANA (*Conolophus spp*)

There are two endemic species of these large, yellowish lizards in the Galápagos. One, *Conolophus pallidus*, lives only on Santa Fé. The other, *Conolophus subcristatus*, has a more reddish-orange hue. It now lives on six of the islands: Fernandina, Isabela, Santa Cruz, South Plaza, Baltra and Seymour. There were once so many iguanas on Santiago that Darwin complained he could find nowhere to pitch his tent, as the ground was undermined by burrows. Today they have all gone. On Baltra, too, the iguanas disappeared during World War II, when the island was occupied by the US military. Luckily Captain Allan Hancock, a wealthy American industrialist, had transferred 72 individuals to neighbouring Seymour in 1932 and so saved the race. Many have since been repatriated to Baltra.

Adult land iguanas are predominantly vegetarian and eat mostly *Opuntia* cactus pads and fruits, spines and all, either on the ground or on plants which droop to within reach of an iguana standing on its hind legs. They also love flowers and readily eat those of the cacti *Sesuvium* and *Portulaca*. Even visitors with any yellow on their person will attract these lumbering reptiles. They also resort to eating carrion when available. Young iguanas begin life eating various insects and arthropods before converting to vegetarianism.

Land iguanas seem to wear a permanent smile and have a rather dim-witted countenance. However, once they have warmed up, their sprinting ability will take anyone by surprise. Land iguanas and giant tortoises have developed a symbiotic relationship with some bird species. When small and medium ground finches or mockingbirds land close to the iguanas or tortoises, or on top of them, the reptiles adopt a bizarre erect posture. This allows the birds unrestricted access to the reptiles' skin, to feed on body ticks and other parasites. Marine iguanas have fewer external parasites living in their watery environment and do not assume this helpful posture, although birds may still remove the parasites they do have.

Large male land iguanas may reach 13kg and more than 1m in length. During breeding, males establish heavily defended territories which overlap with those of up to seven females. When a female becomes receptive she advertises the fact to the male by a raised posture and head shaking, mates with him and disappears to an area suitable to lay her eggs. She will dig a long burrow down to a damp area of soil and deposit up to 20 eggs in the clutch; then aggressively defend her nesting chamber against other females, who are likely to dig it up while looking for a place to deposit their own eggs.

Emerging hatchlings are roughly the size of lava lizards. They immediately come under attack from hordes of predators. Hawks, owls, snakes and herons loiter around the nesting area ready for the bonanza, not to mention a full gamut

Conolophus subcristatus, a land iguana from Urvina Bay, Isabela. (PO)

of introduced mammals. Hatchlings which do survive reach sexual maturity at about 12 years of age, and may go on to live more than 60 years. Without doubt the two best places to observe land iguanas are on the islands of South Plaza and Sante Fé, although the reptiles may also readily be encountered at Urvina Bay and on the hike to Volcán Alcedo, both on Isabela.

MARINE IGUANA (*Amblyrhyncus cristatus*)

No animal is more quintessentially *Galápagueño* than the endemic marine iguana. The only truly marine lizard in the world, it is common throughout the coastline of the archipelago. Growing in excess of 1.5m and weighing up to 13kg, this large, black lizard feeds almost exclusively on marine algae. The larger males, particularly, are able to swim through the surf and dive to a depth of 10m to hang on to the rocks with their powerful claws and graze the algae. The smaller individuals tend not to stray too far from shore, feeding in rock pools and on algae exposed at low tide. Marine iguanas have short snouts (the meaning of *Amblyrhyncus*) and protruding, tricuspid teeth which closely crop the fast-growing seaweed.

Although not truly social, marine iguanas are highly gregarious, often spending the cool nights in clusters several animals deep. Come morning, they

emerge from under vegetation and begin 'charging their batteries' under the rising equatorial sun. Lying flat to expose as much of their black surface as possible to the sun's rays, they are seen at Punta Espinosa on Fernandina in their hundreds, all similarly oriented. Their black colouration may help to absorb the sun's energy and does offer some camouflage,

Above Marine iguanas (*Amblyrhynchus cristatus*) and Sally lightfoot crabs (*Grapsus grapsus*) are two of the most common species to be seen around the coastal tourist trails. (PO)

Above right Though mostly vegetarian, marine iguanas will sometimes feed on animal matter such as a sea lion placenta, as shown. (HB)

particularly for the young animals. As they warm up, they turn to face the sun, and raise their bodies in an elevated basking position which minimises the area of direct radiation while allowing a cooling breeze to circulate under their bellies. Having reached a core temperature of 35.5°C (a fairly typical optimal reptile temperature) or above, the big males are ready to take the plunge into the frigid waters of the Humboldt Current. Specially adapted to retain heat, they immediately lower their heartbeat (bradycardia) to about half, lessening the contact of warm blood with their cold exterior. After an intense bout of feeding they return to shore and spend more time basking. Specially enlarged glands help remove the excess salt from their diet; they eject it forcibly in two plumes of fine spray from their nostrils, rather like a sneeze. If you approach an iguana too quickly it will very likely spray to clear its nostrils in case it has to run away, breathing heavily.

In the marine iguana colonies, mating and egg-laying take place in January–March, which are the hottest months. On several islands the males take on a deep-red colouration which advertises their eagerness to mate. On Española, males turn bright red and turquoise, and females also turn red.

Males set up territories, the preferred areas being above the high-tide mark, which are fiercely contested. Raised triangular scales on tops of the males' heads serve, like deers' antlers, to interlock during bouts of territorial shoving. It is an exhausting period for the males, who may undergo many days of fasting to maintain possession of their 'plot'. Unlike deer, males control only the land and not the females.

Marine iguanas (*Amblyrhynchus cristatus*) are excellent swimmers, holding their legs flush to their body and propelling themselves with powerful strokes of their long flattened tails. (PO)

The dominant males hold areas that females most like to frequent, and therefore mate with more of them. During mating the male grabs the scruff of the female's neck with his mouth, and pins her to the floor with his body. He then inseminates her with one of his two penises. Some five weeks later the females find an area in which to dig a burrow where they lay one to four eggs. Each female actively defends her burrows against other females, and on some islands females turn reddish in colour, adding a mock maleness to their aggressiveness. The breeding season comes to an end, hormones wane and the iguanas return to their ashy black colouration. Three to four months later, hatchlings emerge and are preyed upon heavily, like the land iguanas.

After copulation female lava lizards (*Microlophus spp*) lay eggs in soil. These hatch into tiny miniatures of their parents after about three months. (JRG)

LAVA LIZARDS (*Microlophus spp*)

There are seven endemic species of lava lizards spread out around the archipelago. Six species each live on a single island (Española, San Cristóbal, Floreana, Pinzón, Pinta, Marchena), while the seventh inhabits ten major islands (the remainder except for Genovesa, Darwin and Wolf where there are none). Males are larger than females, the largest individuals being found on Española where they reach 30cm in length, double the length of those on most other islands. Lava lizards are highly predatory, taking any number of arthropods, including centipedes, scorpions, locusts and flies. Sometimes they are even cannabalistic! Very often they can be seen feeding around lounging sea lions, or from a carcass, ambushing the flies they attract.

Females tend to be prettier than males, usually having some red around the head or neck, while males have a more distinct pattern. Males are territorial and often use the trail marker posts to display from. For both threat and courtship, males display by doing a series of push-ups similar to the head-nodding performed by iguanas. The frequency and depth of each push-up is like a Morse code, only understood by members of the same species. Even the females defend territories, but only against other females. Like the iguanas of the Galápagos, they control their body temperature through behaviour. Almost all predators prey on lava lizards.

GECKOS (*Phyllodactylus spp*)

There are at least nine gecko species in Galápagos: three introduced, one native and five endemic. These small (about 12–15cm), common, nocturnal lizards are well known for their ability to cling to smooth surfaces – even upside down. Their secret is that each digit has a splayed-out tip covered in thousands of minute hairs, each ending in a disc-like structure. The hairs wedge into microscopic irregularities on surfaces, giving a strong grip, but to move the lizard must first uncurl its toes. Geckos have very large eyes which they use to hunt their insect prey at night, and a soft skin, more like a toad than a lizard. They lay one single, large, hard-shelled egg at a time, often cementing it to the underside of bark. They are commonly seen at night, particularly by local residents whose homes they share.

SNAKES (*Philodryas sp* and *Alsophis sp*)

Galápagos has three species of endemic snake, plus the yellow-bellied sea snake, *Pelamis platurus*, which occurs occasionally. The endemic snakes have one subspecies or another on all the major islands except the five most northerly, where they never arrived and established. They feed mostly on lava lizards, young marine and land iguanas, and geckos, but will also take some insects, rats and probably young birds. They are only about 1m long and harmless to humans. Most often they are seen in the coastal zones, particularly on Española and Fernandina, often stalking lava lizards.

Galápagos snakes (*Philodryas sp* and *Alsophis sp*) are constrictors. Although they may have a mild venom, they kill their prey by first seizing it in their mouth, and then coiling their body around it. As the prey exhales, the coils tighten, not allowing re-inhalation and so suffocating the prey. (PO)

BIRDS

Waved albatross (*Phoebastria irrorata*) (PO)

The Galápagos Islands have become a very popular destination not only for lovers of general wildlife, but also for hard-core birdwatchers – people who leave footprints on your back when a new bird is spotted. Many of the bird species in the archipelago can be seen nowhere else in the world. Of these endemic species, 22 are land birds, six are seabirds and one, the lava heron, may be described as coastal. Nearly all are readily seen.

The Galápagos archipelago has a land area greater than 8,000km^2. The topography is very varied, ranging from large areas of flat coastline to a high point of 1,707m on Volcán Wolf on Isabela. Within each habitat, from sandy beaches to *scalesia* cloudforest or Pampa zone, different birds have found their ecological niche, thus in order to see the diverse range of avifauna you need to visit as many different habitat types as possible. Different islands, even in close proximity, contain closely related yet different species, a point somewhat overlooked by Darwin during his visit. The serious birdwatcher will therefore wish to plan a trip not only to a range of critical habitats, but to the islands that are home to the birds he or she particularly wishes to see.

Galápagos dove (*Zenaida galapagoensis*) (DH)

Compared with the mainland, there is not a particularly high diversity of species on the Galápagos, and many species which one might expect are absent. There are no hummingbirds, woodpeckers or parrots, for example, all of which are well represented on the mainland. They just never made it. The attractiveness of the birds that are present lies mostly in their tameness. It is quite remarkable that visitors are able to approach, to within a metre, birds sitting on eggs or involved in elaborate courtship rituals, without altering their behaviour. Because of the tropical setting of the Galápagos there is generally very reduced seasonality of breeding, so visitors can see various species breeding during any month of the year. The Galápagos offers a truly intimate look not only at the endemic birds, but also at many other species which are synonymous with the islands, particularly the frigatebirds and boobies.

For the purposes of this book we have divided the birds into three main categories, namely land birds, seabirds and shore birds (including aquatic birds).

LAND BIRDS

O f the 29 species of land birds considered in this chapter, no fewer than 22 are endemic to the Galápagos. They may not be the most glamorous or colourful group, but they are extremely approachable and tame. Undoubtedly the most famous endemic land birds are the 13 species of Darwin's finches, followed by four mockingbirds, a martin, a flycatcher, a dove, a rail and a hawk.

Originally, land birds would have had to travel about 1,000km from the nearest mainland, probably on the heels of a large storm, with individuals or small flocks being blown off course and out to sea, only to alight on the harsh volcanic islands and eventually colonise and speciate here.

MOCKINGBIRDS (*Nesomimus spp*)

There are four species of mockingbirds inhabiting the islands, one on Española, one on San Cristóbal, one on two islets off Floreana and the other on all the major islands except Pinzón and Floreana. They are extremely curious and will often come hopping down the beach to investigate a new landing party. The mockingbirds are omnivorous but show strong predator tendencies, especially those on Española. All of them have browny grey colouration, with long tails and legs and an upright stance. They have long, thin bills, particularly the species on Española, which has a dagger-like bill.

On some islands, mockingbirds (*Nesomimus spp*) have been seen attacking the eggs of boobies. (DH)

DARWIN'S FINCHES

There are 13 species of Darwin's finches in the Galápagos, all small, dull, sparrow-like birds with short tails, rounded wings, rather plump bodies and uninteresting songs. However, Darwin realised that they provided important clues which helped him to generate and later substantiate his theories of evolution. The finches are still evolving, which leads to rather a lot of overlap between certain species and makes identification problematic. Michael Harris, a well-known ornithologist, states of the Galápagos: 'It is only a very wise man or a fool who thinks that he is able to identify all the finches which he sees.' Each species fills a particular niche.

There are six species of ground finches (*Geospiza*): the small, medium, large, sharp-beaked, cactus and large cactus ground finches. Adult males are all black in plumage, while immature and female birds are dull brown with speckled buff breasts. They inhabit the arid lowlands, where they forage for plant matter on the ground or in low bushes. The cactus finches show a preference for cactus seeds, also feeding on the pulp of cactus fruit. Like many of Darwin's finches, the ground finches are hard to tell apart. The main differences are in general beak size and shape. Only by taking accurate measurements of bill length, width and depth, and comparing them with head size, can a scientist cautiously categorise an individual. Beak size and shape is an indication of diet. Heavy bills can crack open large seeds, whereas delicate, tweezer-like bills belong to insect eaters. The vegetarian finch has been classified in a separate genus, *Playtspiza*. The genus of tree finches (*Camarhynchus*), which includes the small, medium and large tree finches along with the mangrove and woodpecker finches, show very little or no black in their plumage and have a more olive-green base colour. They are all arboreal, largely insectivorous and breed from the transition zone upwards, although they do visit the arid zones when not breeding.

Perhaps the most famous of all the Darwin's finches is the woodpecker finch, one of the bird kingdom's rare tool-users. It will actually break off and modify a thin branch or cactus spine and use it to probe into holes in trees and extract wood-boring grubs. It has filled the empty niche held by woodpeckers on the mainland but lacks the long, barbed tongue of its namesake to spear grubs, so has had to revert to improvisation and the use of a tool to extract them. To a lesser extent the mangrove finch uses a similar tool, but is rarely seen, being restricted to less-visited parts of Fernandina and Isabela. The only finch to have a single-island distribution is the medium tree finch, found only on Floreana. Last but not least, the diminutive warbler finch is so unfinch-like that even Darwin had his doubts about it. It behaves almost exactly like a warbler, flitting from bush to bush and searching under leaves for small insects and spiders. Recently the warbler finch has been split into two distinct species on the basis of genetics: a grey warbler finch and a green one. Both have a delicate bill and no black in the plumage.

The breeding in all species is remarkably similar. All Darwin's finches make elaborate dome-shaped nests of twigs, bark and lichens, with a single entrance hole. Very likely the roof is an attempt to create shade from the equatorial sun, but it may also help the finch to defend its nest against would-be predators, particularly snakes. All species are territorial in their breeding, although densities may be as high as one pair per 100m^2.

Above left Warbler finch
(*Certhidea olivacea*) (PO)
Centre left Medium ground finch
(*Geospiza fortis*) (DH)
Below left Small tree finch
(*Camarhynchus parvulus*) (PO)
Above right Cactus finch (*Geospiza scandens*) (DH)
Centre right Large ground finch
(*Geospiza magnirostris*) (PO)
Below right Vegetarian finch
(*Platyspiza crassirostris*) (PO)

The mockingbirds form small family bands, or gangs, which are highly territorial. Gang members feed cooperatively within their territory, although they maintain a strict pecking order. The lower-ranking members of the gang, which are usually offspring of the breeding pairs, help in the duties of raising the young.

Yellow warbler (*Dendroica petechia*), a colourful non-endemic. (PO)

OTHER LAND BIRDS
Yellow warbler (*Dendroica petechia*)
The yellow warbler is not endemic to the islands, enjoying a huge range from Alaska south to Peru. It feeds in a manner similar to the warbler finch and also to the Galápagos flycatchers, but will also feed in the inter-tidal zone. Very conspicuous in its bright yellow plumage, it is common throughout the archipelago. The male has red streaks on the breast and a red cap.

Flycatchers
There are two flycatchers in the islands. The Galápagos flycatcher (*Myiarchus magnirostris*) is endemic and quite common on all the major islands, but rather nondescript, being a dull brown with a yellow breast. The male vermilion flycatcher (*Pyrocephalus rubinus*) is one of those 'must see' birds. A stunning red, it is surely one of the archipelago's most colourful species. It is commonly seen sitting on fence posts in the highlands. In typical flycatcher fashion it 'sallies' after insects, catching them in flight and returning to a favourite perch.

Dark-billed cuckoo and smooth-billed ani
This cuckoo, *Coccyzus melacoryphus*, is probably a relatively recent arrival from the mainland, where it is common. It occurs on most of the larger islands but is seldom seen, as it skulks through thick vegetation. Its length is 28cm, including a very long tail with each tail feather ending in a white tip. The upperparts are a dull grey-brown while the underparts are yellow. Unlike some cuckoos, the species does not parasitise the nests of other birds, but raises its own brood of up to five chicks. It is, however, itself under threat from the smooth-billed ani, *Crotophaga sulcirostris*, a relative, which is out-competing it for food. The ani was very likely introduced in the 1960s by farmers, in the erroneous belief that it would remove ticks from their cattle.

Above Vermilion flycatcher
(*Pyrocephalus rubinus*) (DH)
Right Galápagos flycatcher
(*Myiarchus magnirostris*) (PO)

Galápagos martin

Most common in the highlands of the main islands, this endemic bird (*Progne modesta*) is the only resident of the swallow family in Galápagos. The martin has a length of 15cm, and a uniformly dark colouration. It flies with wings held stiffly, and glides between bouts of rapid wingbeats. It is seldom seen at close quarters and visitors are often unaware of its presence flying overhead. It catches insects on the wing, and nests on rock faces inland.

Galápagos dove (*Zenaida galapagoensis*)

The small, endemic Galápagos dove is common in the arid areas of the main islands. See photo on page 50. On Genovesa there are no carpenter bees, which are normally responsible for pollinating *Opuntia* cactus flowers. The cactus has relaxed its defences through a process of evolution (the spines are now soft and hair-like), allowing doves entry to their flowers to feed. It is now the doves which pollinate the *Opuntia* on Genovesa.

Rail, crake and moorhen

The tiny (15cm) endemic Galápagos rail (*Laterallus spilonotus*) is common in the moist highlands of some of the major islands, but is seldom, if ever, seen by the normal visitor. Like the native paint-billed crake, *Neocrex erythrops*, it is a highly secretive (although approachable) skulking bird that is reluctant to fly, and would rather dash off into the undergrowth if danger threatens.

The much larger moorhen or common gallinule (*Gallinula chloropus*) is a more visible species that prefers brackish water and inland lakes. Not too exciting for the birdwatcher, this has one of the largest world ranges of any bird, so is probably more easily seen at home.

The Galápagos hawk (*Buteo galapagoensis*) is entirely diurnal and is the top natural predator in Galápagos. (DH)

Raptors

Three raptor species have come to live in Galápagos: the endemic barn owl (*Tyto punctatissima*), the short-eared owl (*Asio flammeus galapagoensis*) and the endemic Galápagos hawk (*Buteo galapagoensis*). The least often seen is the barn owl, which is entirely nocturnal, feeding mostly on rats, mice and insects. It is 26cm in length with a white, heart-shaped face and underparts, and a pale tan back. Probably the best place to find one is at the entrance to a lava tunnel on Santa Cruz, or in a farm building in the highlands.

The short-eared owl is sighted much more often. On Genovesa, particularly, it is commonly seen at the storm petrel colony where it hunts, on foot, by waiting at a storm petrel burrow entrance, and suddenly lunging its legs and claws into the hole when it hears a bird within reach. Although it does eat mammals, it takes many more birds, of several species, than the barn owl does. It nests

Where there are no Galápagos hawks on an island (such as Genovesa and Santa Cruz) the short-eared owl (*Asio flammeus*) does not suffer any competition and boldly hunts in daylight. (PO)

on the ground, well hidden in thick vegetation. Larger than the barn owl at up to 42cm in length, the short-eared owl is much browner with dark streaks on both the upper and under surfaces. Its ears are small and often hard to see.

Galápagos hawks are so tame that they will even land on people's heads! This bird is one of the world's rarest raptors, with up to 150 'pairs' and about 800 individuals living in the islands, making it vulnerable as a species. The hawks are very commonly seen on most major islands and are unmistakable: juveniles rather cream-coloured, adults a dark chocolate-brown. At 56cm, females are larger than males. The species has evolved with a breeding system called cooperative polyandry, whereby the female mates with up to four males and all then help her raise the chicks (up to three in a clutch).

Apart from hunting anything from iguanas and snakes to rats and birds, the hawks are also the major scavengers of the islands, feeding on any rotting carcass – their favourite is goat.

SEABIRDS

S eabirds are defined as those species which make some or most of their living from the open sea. There are four main groupings of seabirds in the world: the *Sphenisciformes* which are the penguins, the *Procellariformes* which are the tube-nosed birds such as albatrosses and storm petrels, the *Pelecaniformes* which include frigatebirds, tropicbirds, boobies and cormorants, and the *Charadriiformes* which include the gulls, terns and waders.

True seabirds are a very special group of highly adapted species. The ocean is basically a desert – as the Ancient Mariner said, 'Water, water, everywhere, nor any drop to drink.' We, as mammals, suffer severe dehydration if we drink seawater, as our kidneys cannot deal with the high concentration of salts, and excess body fluids are used up trying to get rid of them. Seabirds, like marine iguanas, have evolved large, active salt glands that act as an extra set of 'super kidneys'. These are situated in the depression on top of the skull. When the blood becomes loaded with salts caused by the intake of seawater, it is shunted to the head and passes through the salt gland which acts as a desalination plant, leaving useful fresh water in the blood. The concentrated salt solution is expelled from the gland via the nostrils (as a spray in the marine iguanas). Some birds have grooves or tubes on the bill to channel the solution, which can be seen dripping from the bill-tips of birds recently returning ashore. In another effort to conserve fresh water, the nitrogen wastes of the body are not dissolved in water to form urea, but are further processed to form uric acid, a thick white paste (guano). The salt gland means that seabirds are not tied to the land, except during breeding. The sight of a pelagic seabird on the open ocean, such as a diminutive storm petrel or a regal albatross, reminds me of another quote from Coleridge's *Rime of the Ancient Mariner*: 'Alone, alone, all, all alone, Alone on a wide wide sea!'

GALÁPAGOS PENGUIN (*Spheniscus mendiculus*)

It seems incongruous to find penguins on the Equator. Indeed, the endemic Galápagos penguin is the only penguin to nest entirely within the tropics, and also, in the case of those living on the northern tip of Isabela, the only one to nest naturally within the northern hemisphere. The Galápagos penguin is the third-smallest penguin in the world, standing only 30cm or so tall. Like the other members of the *Spheniscus* group (the jackass, Humboldt and Magellanic penguins) they are black and white, and nest in burrows. With no soft peat to make burrows for themselves, Galápagos penguins have taken to living in natural caves and crevices in the coastal lava. They mainly occur in the cooler waters around Isabela and Fernandina islands, and recently nesting pairs have been found on Floreana and Bartolomé. Most visitors, however, will see, and swim with, penguins around the base of Pinnacle Rock on Bartolomé.

On shore, Galápagos penguins (*Spheniscus mendiculus*) are easy to spot from a distance, their white bellies standing out against the dark lava. When approached they often turn their backs, making them harder to spot as they blend in with the rock. (PO)

Female penguins lay one or two eggs which are incubated for a period of 35–40 days. The dark-brown chick fledges eight to nine weeks later. Adults mate for life, and in optimal conditions can breed more than once a year.

Although penguins cannot fly in air, they do 'fly' underwater (see photo page 96). Galápagos is one of the few places where a snorkeller can comfortably watch their underwater antics. Penguins may even use the swimmer as a barrier against which to herd a school of fish. These extremely streamlined birds can sprint at speeds of up to 35km/h. During courtship they frequently explode into a very loud, raucous, donkey-like braying. Any moulting penguin, chick or adult, should not be approached lest it be frightened into the water, since penguins' usually excellent insulation becomes ineffective during moulting and they may suffer hypothermia!

BOOBIES

Three species of booby are resident in Galápagos; none is endemic. The blue-footed, red-footed and Nazca booby are members of the *Sulidae* family, which includes gannets. Boobies are strong fliers, sometimes feeding many kilometres offshore, and preying mostly on fish which they catch with spectacular plunge dives. Boobies have forward-pointing, stereoscopic vision which allows them to judge distance accurately and pinpoint their prey, even underwater. This forward-looking aspect of their eyes gives them a rather comical appearance ('booby' refers to the Spanish word *bobo*, meaning clown or stupid). When boobies spot fish, they wheel in the air until they are directly above their prey, then plummet downwards before folding in their wings. They hit the water at the speed of an arrow from a height of about 20m, and grab the unsuspecting fish before it has time to flee. Just prior to impact, the nictitating membrane (a third translucent eyelid) sweeps across from the front of the eye to help protect the eyeball. The prey is usually swallowed before the bird bobs to the surface, to avoid it being stolen by the piratical frigatebirds. In order to prevent two high-powered jets of water from entering the nostrils and

Blue-footed boobies (*Sula nebouxii excisa*) perform an elaborate 'high-step', showing off their incredibly blue feet. (PO)

piercing the brain during a dive, the nostrils are shielded by horny deflector plates on the bill. The three species of booby in Galápagos are able to co-exist, having divided up the resources so they do not compete with each other.

Blue-footed booby
(*Sula nebouxii excisa*)

The blue-footed booby is one of the archipelago's most sought-after birds, not because it is rare but because it is entertaining. Everyone who visits the islands will certainly see it. Their plunge-diving abilities are phenomenal, and it is spectacular to watch a flock dive, in synchrony, on to a school of fish. They are inshore feeders, the males particularly, diving in water sometimes only half a metre deep. When conditions are favourable, they are able to raise three young. As they feed so close to shore, it is feasible for the parent birds to return with food sufficient for three hungry chicks.

Although by far the least common of the three boobies in Galápagos, the blue-foots are the most often seen, as their many small colonies are spread throughout the archipelago. They nest close to shore on flat areas. The nests are relatively closely spaced, but consist of nothing more than a shallow scrape in the ground. Blue-foots have a less than annual breeding cycle, and different colonies can be found breeding around the archipelago throughout the year. Their courtship antics are very entertaining.

Sexes are best differentiated by the eyes. Males appear to have smaller pupils than females. (Females have a darkly stained iris, giving the impression of a larger pupil.) The female is larger and her voice is distinct – she honks, he whistles. In trying to attract a mate, the male actually dances. If attracted, a female will come to join him and together they dance the 'booby two-step'. If all goes well the dance peaks in mutual skypointing, face to face, and culminates in mating. A few presents of stones or twigs are offered in the ceremony, reminders of the days when these birds must have been nest-builders. The incubation period is 41 days; chicks fledge 105 days later.

Above The dancing of a pair of blue-footed boobies (*Sula nebouxii excisa*) is punctuated by a dramatic skypoint. Everything pointed (wingtips, tail and bill) is stretched skyward, accompanied by a long whistle from the male and honk from the female. (PO)

Below A blue-footed booby creates a circular 'nest' in a ring of guano. (DH)

Red-footed booby (*Sula sula websteri*)
The red-foots are distributed in only five main colonies around the archipelago. These are situated on the outer islands close to deep, oceanic water, their preferred feeding area. Although the most numerous booby in Galápagos (Genovesa has the world's largest red-footed 'boobery' – about 140,000 pairs) the species is not often seen unless an actual colony is visited. Red-foots are the smallest boobies and, partly because they may feed hundreds

Left In Galápagos there are two colour types of red-footed boobies (*Sula sula websteri*), white and brown. White ones represent about 5% of the population in Galápagos, a situation which is reversed in the rest of the world. (PO)

Below The red-footed boobies' prehensile feet are able to grip branches, allowing the birds to nest off the ground. (PO)

of kilometres offshore, only manage to bring back enough food to raise a single chick. Unlike Nazca boobies, they lay one egg. Their attempts to raise young are further complicated by the marauding frigatebirds which hang around the colonies and often steal the catch from returning parent birds. Red-foots incubate their egg for 45 days and the chick fledges after 130 days.

Young red-foots in particular often come to investigate boats approaching their island colonies, and show off their perching ability by landing on the rigging and rails. At sea they are true masters of their environment. They have learnt to accompany ships and feed on flying fish which the vessels disturb. In a display of fast low-level flying, red-foots snatch the fish in mid-air.

The Nazca booby (*Sula granti*) is the largest booby in the Galápagos. These are handsome birds which will very likely be seen by all visitors to the islands. (PO)

Nazca booby (*Sula granti*)

In most respects except size, Nazca (masked) boobies are intermediate between the blue-footed and the red-footed booby. They are also plunge-divers, but feed further afield than the blue-foots, in the inter-island area. Compared with blue-foots they have fewer large colonies, but are also widespread throughout the archipelago. The sexes are similar and, like the blue-foots, pairs nest on the ground, usually near a cliff edge. It is interesting that masked boobies lay two eggs but only ever raise one chick. The eggs are laid a few days apart; giving the first chick a distinct advantage over the second. As soon as the second chick hatches, its stronger sibling attacks it and pushes it out of the guano ring which represents the nest. The parents ignore the battle, known as obligate sibling murder (or 'the Cain and Abel syndrome'), and leave the chick to its fate – invariably an attack by mockingbirds. Should the first egg not hatch, the second egg fulfills its role as an insurance and goes on to reach maturity. The incubation period is 40 days; the chick fledges after 115 days.

FRIGATEBIRDS

Five species of frigatebird exist worldwide. Two inhabit the Galápagos: the magnificent frigatebird (*Fregata magnificens*), and the great frigatebird (*Fregata minor*). These giant flying machines have the largest wingspan-to-bodyweight ratio of any bird, making them highly manoeuvrable and acrobatic fliers. Often called man o' war birds, they are notorious as piratical cleptomaniacs that steal food from other birds at every opportunity. This reputation is justified, but frigatebirds are also capable of an 'honest' living.

It would seem that a frigatebird can discriminate between a bird with a full gullet and one which is empty. An unlucky booby or tropicbird may be plucked out of the air, dangled by the tail-tip and shaken until it regurgitates its food, which the frigatebird then makes off with.

Both species of frigatebird are easy to see breeding in Galápagos, the best places being Genovesa, Seymour and San Cristóbal. 'Magnificent' is slightly larger than 'great'. Adult males of the two species are almost impossible to distinguish in flight. At rest, the magnificent boasts a purple sheen on his long back feathers, while the great frigatebird male has an iridescent bottle-green sheen. Females are more readily distinguished; the white on the chest of the female great reaches right up to her chin, while the female magnificent frigatebird has a black throat. The female magnificent has a blue eye-ring; the female great is red.

When ready to breed (timings vary around the archipelago) the male frigatebird first finds a suitable nesting area. Then slowly, over 20 minutes, he pumps air into his grossly exaggerated, bright red, throat pouch until it is the size of a party balloon. As soon as an adult female of his species flies by, he loses control and erupts into fits of rapturous head-shaking and vibrating, while uttering a shrill, high-pitched cry. This spectacle often attracts rival males into the display arena. If the female is suitably impressed she will alight beside him and, with his wing jealously protecting her, the pair bond is sealed.

After mating, a single white egg is laid on the hard guano pad of an old nest in a low bush or tree. The nests are extremely flimsy. Many eggs and even chicks simply fall through the nest and are lost while the parents are changing

Above Male great frigatebird (*Fregata minor*) with fully inflated pouch. Both species of frigatebird possess this extraordinary aid to courtship. (PO)

Left Only a single frigatebird is reared. (DH)

Above A pair of great frigatebirds (*Fregata minor*). (PO)

Below The magnificent frigatebird (*Fregata magnificens*) female has a black chin, unlike the great frigatebird female (above right). She also has a blue eye-ring, not a red one. (PO)

incubation shifts or when twigs are stolen by other frigatebirds. The average incubation stint is about ten days, by the end of which the adults look tired, heat-stricken and lethargic under the noonday equatorial sun. The chick is reliant on the adult for food for up to a year or more, even though it is able to fly about five to six months after hatching. This long dependency period precludes the adults from breeding every year, so they can manage to raise one chick only every two years.

GALÁPAGOS FLIGHTLESS CORMORANT
(*Phalacrocorax harrisi*)
The endemic, flightless cormorant is the largest of the world's 29 cormorant species, and the only one to have lost the power of flight. There are fewer than 1,000 pairs, all living on the coasts of Isabela (mostly in the west and northwest) and Fernandina. They remain extremely localised to their place of birth and many never range more than a few kilometres from their natal shore.

Although they cannot fly, cormorants retain vestigial wings which help them to balance when jumping from rock to rock. As they do not produce

The naked chicks of the flightless cormorant (*Phalacrocorax harrisi*) begin life very ugly, but soon develop a downy brown coat and more resemble the adults. They have voracious appetites and thrust their heads down the throats of their parents to feed. (PO)

The male, flightless cormorant (*Phalacrocorax harrisi*) is slightly larger than the female. Each time he returns to his mate on the nest, he brings an offering of seaweed. She gratefully accepts and adds it to the increasing nest mound. (PO)

much oil to waterproof their feathers, their waterlogged, vestigial wings must be held out to dry after returning to shore, in the classic cormorant pose. Underwater, rather than 'flying' as the penguins do, cormorants keep their wings held close to their sides and kick with their powerful webbed feet, using their long, flexible necks as they delve their heads into holes in search of octopus or eels which they skewer with their heavy, hooked bills. Cormorants sit very low in the water, with not much more than the head and neck visible from a distance. Some lucky visitors witness their elaborate aquatic courtship dance. The male and female birds interlock their necks and utter low guttural calls while twirling around in a tight circle. Nests are untidy affairs, constructed in a mound of seaweed, flotsam and jetsam. They are never more than a few metres from the water's edge, and are continually enhanced. Usually three white eggs are laid, and incubated by both partners. When the chicks hatch after 35 days the partners also rotate feeding duties. Young cormorants do not develop the arresting turquoise eyes of the adults until their second year.

RED-BILLED TROPICBIRD (*Phaethon aethereus*)

Tropicbird colonies are widespread around the archipelago, South Plaza and Genovesa being particularly good places to admire them. During courtship the two birds fly tightly together, until one suddenly stops flapping. Gliding with its wings held in a deep 'v', it lets out a shrill, piercing whistle, hence its nickname, the bosun bird, after the sound made by a bosun's whistle. These birds are plunge-divers, feeding far out to sea. They fall from a great height and grasp the prey in their powerful, serrated, coral-red bill.

Top Red-billed tropicbirds (*Phaethon aethereus*) lay a single egg in their cliff nest hole. The chick has a yellow bill and more black in the plumage than its parents. The characteristic long tail streamers develop only when adult. (DH)

Above Tropicbirds take their Latin name from Phaethon, the son of the Greek god Helios, who attempted to drive the chariot of the sun. Their long, white tail streamers are immediately striking. (JRG)

WAVED ALBATROSS (*Phoebastria irrorata*)

Most experts consider the waved albatross to be endemic to the Galápagos, but there are a few pairs which nest on Isla de la Plata near the Ecuadorian mainland. The rest (approximately 12,000 pairs) breed only on the island of Española in the Galápagos. Part of the colony (at Punta Suárez) is accessible from the visitor site, but the birds are only present between about April and December.

It is incredible to sit near a pair of waved albatross and witness their flamboyant courtship rituals. Returning to Española after months or even years at sea, the birds begin to find their partners of the previous year or, if they are young birds, a mate – for life. Soon after coming ashore, the adult birds begin courting. The ritual between partners is gradually perfected until it becomes a complex series of repeated displays. Visitors sit in awe as the huge birds face each other and go through the motions of 'bill-circling', 'sky-pointing', the 'shy look', the 'drunken swagger', 'bill clapping', 'mooing' and 'gaping'. The movements flow into one another, and are repeated in different orders and punctuated by rest periods, only to begin again.

The culmination is, of course, mating, and eventually (in mid-April to June) a large, 285g, white egg is laid in a shallow scrape directly on the ground. Both birds

A pair of waved albatross (*Phoebastria irrorata*) remains monogamous, barring accidents or death of their 'loved ones', through their long lives of up to 40 years or more. The courtship ritual must therefore create a strong enough pair bond between the partners to last from one year to the next. (DH)

share incubation duties, sometimes remaining a week or more at a time. Finally, some 60 days later, a 200g chick hatches. At this stage in its life, the chick is extremely ugly, really nothing more than a brown, expandable, down-covered sack.

Adults manufacture a substance called chick oil in the proventriculus, part of the stomach. This oil is made from processed squid and crustacea which they have caught at sea. Come feeding time, the chick gently begs from the adult and is rewarded by a mouth-to-mouth transfer of up to 2kg of chick oil, sprayed down its throat in a single feeding. The chick swells visibly, can no longer stand and waddles to some shade to digest its meal. By five months it weighs 2kg more than its parents, but soon loses weight as it begins growing its flight feathers.

Between 24 and 30 weeks after hatching, the young bird is ready to fly. In order to do so it must negotiate the boulder-strewn terrain of Española and walk, clumsily, down a natural 'runway' to a take-off position at the edge of the cliff. In one brave moment, the bird is transformed from a gangly, awkward, earth-bound creature into an elegant flight expert as it leaps into the wind and the unknown, not to return to land for at least the next four years of its life.

OTHER TUBE-NOSED BIRDS
Galápagos shearwater (*Puffinus subalaris*)
Recent research indicates that the Galápagos shearwater is an endemic species in its own right, and not a subspecies of the Audubon shearwater as was previously thought. The population of about 10,000 pairs is thriving and is not endangered. A small shearwater with black upperparts and white beneath, the bird flies in large flocks, often just skimming the surface of the sea.

Galápagos petrel (*Pterodroma phaeopygia*)
Related to the albatrosses, shearwaters and storm petrels, the Galápagos petrel is in critical danger due to predation of chicks and eggs by introduced black rats. It is also the only true petrel to reside in the islands. No census of the current population is available, but the largest colony in the islands, at Cerro Pajas on Floreana, is thought to have around 2,000 pairs. The birds nest in burrows in the highlands of some main islands. The Galápagos petrel is often seen at sea, its conspicuous white forehead glinting in the sunlight as it banks high and glides over the ocean.

Storm petrels
Related to the giant albatross, storm petrels are the smallest seabirds in the world (only 15–20cm in length). The name petrel is derived from Peter as in St Peter, after their dainty ability to 'walk' on water. Fluttering like butterflies, they gently patter along the water surface, creating tiny currents which drag floating food particles towards them. They are commonly seen at sea in the wake of vessels, feeding on discarded spoils from the ship's galley.

Three species breed in the islands: the white-vented storm petrel (*Oceanites gracilis*), the band-rumped storm petrel (*Oceanodroma castro*) and the wedge-rumped (Galápagos) storm petrel (*Oceanodroma tethys*). All are small, black birds with varying degrees of white on their rumps. One of the best places to watch storm petrels *en masse* is above Prince Philip's Steps on Genovesa. Here, hundreds of thousands of wedge-rumped petrels nest. They can be seen by day, flitting like gnats a few metres above the broken lava field in which they nest. Females lay their single egg in the network of cracks and interstices in the lava, to gain protection from the predatory short-eared owl. Storm petrels have an incredible olfactory sense and, despite their huge numbers, are able to detect their burrow entrance by smell. The white-vented storm petrel, although a common resident of the islands and often seen inshore, still withholds a major secret. To date no nests of this species have been found!

GULLS

Only two species of gull breed in the archipelago: the lava gull, which is endemic, and the swallow-tailed gull, which is also restricted to Galápagos apart from a few breeding pairs on Malpelo Island (Colombia). The two species show many similarities, though not in their behaviour. Three other species show up in the islands occasionally: the laughing gull, the kelp gull, and Franklin's gull, the latter being much more common. All are rather nondescript black and white gulls, setting them apart from the more handsome Galápagos natives.

Lava gull (*Larus fuliginosus*)

Despite their wide, albeit sparse, distribution, the solitary nests of lava gulls are extremely hard to find. The most memorable feature of these gulls is the bright red gape, which is displayed during their raucous, frequently heard 'long calls'. The mouth colouration contrasts with the dark, ash-grey plumage of the adults. The juveniles are a uniform brown.

Swallow-tailed gull (*Larus furcatus*)

The swallow-tailed gull is unlike most other gulls in many ways. First, it is the world's only nocturnal, truly oceanic gull. At dusk, it flies many kilometres out to sea to feed. To aid in their nocturnal foraging, these gulls possess more rods than cones in their eyes' retinas (to pick up black and white contrast as opposed to colour). They also rely on the natural bioluminescent light given off by their favourite prey – squid. They will nest on sand or lava, but their preferred nesting habitat is sea cliff. To prevent themselves crashing into the cliff walls on their return in darkness, they utter clicking vocalisations, thought to be a form of primitive echo-location, similar to that of bats. They have a less-than-annual breeding cycle, so various stages of egg and chick growth can be seen in any colony at any one time. After courtship, which involves food gifts from the male, it is he who selects the nest site. The female lays a single egg on a crude nest built of assorted pebbles and coral fragments. The young chick hatches as a cryptic ball of down, the target of predators such as frigatebirds and short-eared owls (especially on Genovesa).

Above The lava gull (*Larus fuliginosus*) is possibly the planet's rarest gull with only about 400 pairs in the world. It is fairly sedentary in its habits and is a true scavenger, often seen close to human settlements. (DH)

Below The large eye of this swallow-tailed gull (*Larus furcatus*) is typical of a nocturnal animal. The bright red, fleshy eye ring, however, has no known function. (PO)

BROWN PELICAN (*Pelecanus occidentalis urinator*)

Relatives of frigatebirds, pelicans put their pouches to practical rather than ornamental use. Indeed, some experts speculate that the pelican's pouch may have evolved as a defence against frigatebird piracy. Brown pelicans are the smallest of their family, and the only pelicans which are truly marine, also the only ones (including the Peruvian subspecies) which plunge-dive to catch their food. On impact they lunge rather awkwardly, half-twisting on to their backs as they strike underwater with their long necks. As they lunge at prey their pouch distends grossly, trapping up to 13 litres of water and, with luck, some fish. As the pelican lifts its head from the water, the water drains out, the pouch contracts and the fish are swallowed. Brown noddy terns (*Anous stolidus*, opposite) can often be seen perching on the pelicans' heads waiting to snap up any small morsels which escape the pouch. Brown pelicans nest in many scattered colonies throughout most of the archipelago. Breeding occurs in any month, although particular colonies are synchronised.

Brown pelicans (*Pelecanus occidentalis urinator*) make large, untidy nests of twigs on low bushes and mangroves, and lay two to three white eggs. (JRG)

Brown noddies (*Anous stolidus*) are small, brown terns with large, wedge-shaped tails and white foreheads; the bird pictured is a juvenile. Wherever there is a mêlée of feeding fish and birds, the noddies are sure to be seen plucking small fish from the surface. The name noddy is derived from their habit of nodding to each other during courtship. They lay a single egg on bare rock, usually under an overhang on a low sea cliff. (PO)

PHALAROPES

Three phalarope species frequent the Galápagos Islands: the northern or (red-necked) *Phalaropus lobatus*, the grey (or red) *Phalaropus fulicarius*, and the Wilson's phalarope, *Phalaropus tricolor*. Part of the *Charadriiformes* group, phalaropes are not typical seabirds but rather waders. By far the most common is the northern phalarope, which nests in the high arctic and subarctic tundra. All phalaropes are strongly migratory, and are the only waders to be seen on the ocean surface in the Galápagos. Between August and April, particularly around Christmas, there are huge flocks of them. These small (20–24cm) birds with thin, straight bills and an upright posture appear in the Galápagos in their black and white, non-breeding plumage. They have well-developed salt glands, lobed and partly-webbed toes and a dense plumage which traps a lot of air, causing them to bob high on the water like a cork. They swim rather jerkily and spin on the surface, creating tiny whirlpools which suck in the plankton on which they partly feed. Interestingly, phalaropes show reversal in their breeding patterns. The female is larger than the male and more brightly coloured. He needs camouflage, for it is he who incubates the eggs.

SHORE BIRDS

Many resident shore birds of the Galápagos are now sufficiently different from mainland species to have been awarded an endemic subspecies status by taxonomists. Only one has been given full species status: the endemic lava heron, *Butorides sundevalli*. Two other herons, the yellow-crowned night heron, *Nyctanassa violacea*, and the great blue heron, *Ardea herodias*, have been recognised as endemic subspecies, as has the Galápagos white-cheeked pintail (*Anas bahamensis galapagensis*).

HERONS
Great blue heron (*Ardea herodias*)
The largest of the Galápagos herons, the great blue heron is an efficient and voracious predator which feeds on a variety of marine organisms, including young marine iguanas and turtle hatchlings. Particularly on Fernandina, I have often watched great blue herons seizing young marine iguana hatchlings, carrying them to water to wash them and then devouring them whole. They lay two to three eggs in a bulky nest on top of mangroves, and can be found nesting on most of the larger islands.

Yellow-crowned night herons (*Nyctanassa violacea*) can be seen on many of the islands, standing stoically, often on one leg, waiting for darkness. (DH)

Yellow-crowned night heron (*Nyctanassa violacea*)
As their name suggests, these birds are primarily nocturnal hunters. One of the easiest places to see them is around the base of streetlights in Port Ayora on Santa Cruz, where they feed on locusts, centipedes, scorpions and even young rats. Occasionally they hunt also in daylight, particularly favouring the sally lightfoot crabs which scuttle over the lava rocks. These are predominantly solitary birds that nest in rock crevices or in low bushes, and lay three to four eggs. A more natural place to observe them is in Darwin Bay on Genovesa.

The great blue heron (*Ardea horodias*) is similar to species in North America and Europe. (PO)

The only endemic heron of the Galápagos, the lava heron (*Butorides sundevalli*) is commonly seen as it stands quietly beside a rock pool, blending beautifully into its surroundings. The juvenile seen here is easily confused with the striated heron. (DH)

Lava heron (*Butorides sundevalli*)

Lava herons feed in the characteristic fashion of a 'sit-and-wait' predator, maintaining a fabulous sense of alertness and concentration. The all-dark adult plumage distinguishes the lava heron from the very similar striated heron (*Butorides striatus*), which is a little less common throughout the islands and has a brown-streaked plumage, a green back and a black cap. Lava herons lay one to three eggs in rocky crevices or in mangrove stands.

Egrets

Three egret species occur on the islands: the great egret (*Casmerodius albus*), the snowy egret (*Egretta thula*), and the cattle egret (*Bubulcus ibis*), in order of descending size. All are fairly recent colonists and are highly conspicuous with their bright white plumage. The cattle egret is the only heron that breeds during its first year and the only bird species to have reached all seven continents. The vagrant snowy egret is occasionally found in small numbers along the coast.

OTHER SHORE BIRDS

The Galápagos Islands are home to a number of shore and water birds, and a stopping-off place for many other migratory species such as oystercatchers, stilts, turnstones, plovers, whimbrels, sandpipers and phalaropes (see page 75).

In 1968 as many as 2,000 white-cheeked pintails (*Anas bahamensis galapagoensis*) were killed when a caldera collapsed on Fernandina, and thousands of tons of rock fell into the caldera lake. (PO)

Galápagos white-cheeked pintail (*Anas bahamensis galapagoensis*)

The white-cheeked pintail is a fairly common duck around the islands, occurring on any body of fresh or salt water. It is mostly vegetarian but will also take invertebrates, and can be seen up-ending in shallow water to feed. This species nests on the ground among waterside vegetation such as mangrove roots. The female will lay up to ten eggs in a clutch.

Wandering tattler (*Heteroscelus incanus*)

This common visitor (28cm in length) to the Galápagos shoreline is a non-resident. It migrates from its breeding grounds in the North American tundra to winter in Galápagos. Wandering tattlers can be seen chasing the receding waves to feed on small invertebrates. When standing, they

Black-necked stilts (*Himantopus himantopus*) are common on freshwater lagoons. They feed on tiny organisms, plucking them from the mud or water with their fine, forcep-like bills. (DH)

A conspicuous shore bird, the American oystercatcher (*Haematopus palliatus*) is often heard before it is seen. Its loud, shrill call directs the eye over the bare lava to a handsome black and white bird with a striking orange bill. (PO)

have a rather comical, characteristic bob. These birds are usually seen alone. They have dark grey upperparts, with paler underparts and yellow legs.

American oystercatcher (*Haematopus palliatus*)

Oystercatchers make their living in the inter-tidal zone, feeding on crustaceans and molluscs. They are able to open crab shells with their strong beaks and eat the contents. Their nest is nothing more than a scrape above the high-tide mark. Two eggs are laid which hatch two precocial chicks (young that, like baby chickens, are able to be up and about and following their parents immediately).

Caribbean flamingo (*Phoenicopterus ruber*)

Named after the phoenix, a mythical bird that consumed itself by fire to rise again from the ashes, these stunning birds indeed look like living flames within the black and ashy surroundings of their home.

Quietly filtering the brackish waters, the birds spread between the major lagoons of the archipelago, particularly those on Floreana, Isabela, Rábida, Santiago, Santa Cruz and Bainbridge Rocks. They seem to undertake unseasonal migrations from lagoon to lagoon, on an individual basis, according to local food abundance. Inside their bills are a series of plates which serve to strain tiny invertebrate food organisms from the water and mud. The tongue acts as a piston, drawing water in through the front of the bill and then forcing it out of the sides,

There are probably fewer than 500 individual Caribbean flamingos (*Phoenicopterus ruber*) within the archipelago. This fragile population should be approached with extreme sensitivity, particularly during the breeding season, as the birds will desert their nests if disturbed. (PO)

The down-curved bill of the Caribbean flamingo (*Phoenicopterus ruber*) is held upside down and parallel to the water surface when in the feeding position. (JRG)

past the plates. These birds often patter their feet in the mud to disturb food, but may also feed in deep water – they can swim very well if necessary.

Flamingos build rather elaborate, cone-shaped domes, like mini volcanoes, at the lake edge, and lay a single egg. Less than a week after hatching, the dull grey, stubby, straight-billed chick leaves the nest to join other chicks in a crêche, watched over by a few adult birds. The bill gradually curves, the legs lengthen and eventually the young take on a pinkish hue derived from the carotenoid pigments of their diet. Courtship is a busy time at a colony, as the brightly coloured adults dance noisily in the lagoons.

Mammals

A sea lion (*Zalophus wollebaeki*) relaxes
on a rock, San Cristóbal. (PO)

Sea lions (*Zalophus wollebaeki*) are superbly adapted to their aquatic lifestyle, with excellent underwater vision. They also have evolved directional underwater hearing which helps them to locate their prey. (JRG)

SEA LIONS

The pinnipeds (flippered feet) comprise 33 species around the world, divided into three groups: true seals (*Phocidae*), eared seals (*Otaridae*) and walruses (*Odobenidae*). Galápagos has two species of eared seals, both endemic: the recently declared endemic offshoot of the Californian sea lion (*Zalophus wollebaeki*) and the Galápagos fur seal (*Arctocephalus galapagoensis*). Galápagos therefore has no 'true' seals.

The eared seals are characterised by external ear pinnae, by the ability to rotate their hind flipper under their pelvic girdle and by their long, flipper-like front limbs. True seals have heavy claws on their front limbs which are very hand-like. Unlike eared seals, true seals must shuffle along on their pelvic girdles like huge maggots, with their hind flippers always trailing. Eared seals on the other hand can gallop – even out-running a person on rocky terrain! When swimming, eared seals use their fore flippers simultaneously for propulsion and their hind flippers as rudders, while true seals use their fore

Unlike true seals, sea lions (*Zalophus wollebaeki*) and fur seals (*Arctocephalus galapagoensis*) are able to lift their bodies clear of the ground. They walk either in a typical quadruped gait or in a true gallop. (PO)

flippers as rudders, and their hind flippers in an alternate sculling motion. Usually associated with cold environments, the two Galápagos seals have the most tropical distribution of any pinnipeds in the world.

Probably the strongest memory of any visitor to the islands is the delight felt when swimming and interacting with these two intelligent mammals.

GALÁPAGOS SEA LION (*Zalophus wollebaeki*)

There is a large degree of sexual dimorphism (differences between the sexes apart from genitalia) in sea lions. Males weigh up to 250kg while females reach only 100kg. There are approximately 16,000 individuals throughout the archipelago, a number which has decreased over the last decade. Sea lions like to haul out on sandy beaches. The best places to see them are probably Plaza Sur, Isla Mosquera, Gardner Bay on Española, Rábida and Puerto Egas on Santiago.

Males establish territories which are savagely defended from rivals and interlopers, forcing the unsuccessful bulls to leave the area and set up bachelor colonies away from the female haul-outs. Reproduction occurs mostly in the *garúa* season (July to December) although this varies from island to island.

Sea lion pups (*Zalophus wollebaeki*) learn to swim at about one to two weeks of age, usually in shallow, rocky pools in safe nursery areas. (DH)

Above A female sea lion (*Zalophus wollebaeki*) fends off a hawk which has come in to feed on its afterbirth. Hawks have been known to attack newborn pups as well. (JRG)

Below A sea lion (*Zalophus wollebaeki*) relaxing. (PO)

Three to four weeks after pupping, the female comes back into oestrus and the bull copulates with her. As in the fur seal, there is a system of delayed implantation, whereby the fertilised egg floats in the uterus for approximately two months before implanting. After the single pup is born (rarely twins) the mother stays with it for the first week and completes the pair bond, both by vocalisation and by smell. Then she begins to forage by day, returning to suckle in the evenings. At five weeks old, the pups moult their baby coat or lanugo, to look more like miniature adults. By about five months old the pup will begin feeding inshore for itself but may be dependent on its mother a lot longer.

Bulls are polygamous and make little or no parental investment. They do not maintain a true harem, simply defend an area of beach. The dominant bull has the territory most favoured by the females, so (like the marine iguanas) is able to mate with more females than a less dominant bull.

Sea lions are highly thigmotactic (they seek body contact) and loaf around in piles on the beach. They are extremely efficient hunters, preferring sardines to other fish, so spend a considerable time resting or at play. Underwater they are extremely well streamlined, lithe and acrobatic. Only the bulls should be avoided – they are easily recognised, not only by their large size, but by the pronounced bump on their forehead. The young are highly inquisitive and it is not unusual for them to nibble on a snorkeller's flippers while swimming. Serious injuries can be inflicted by the bulls, and they should be given the distance and respect they seek.

Bull sea lion (*Zalophus wollebaeki*). The prominent bump on the forehead makes it easy to tell males from females. (DH)

Once hunted almost to extinction, the population of Galápagos fur seals
(*Arctocephalus galapagoensis*) is once again alarmingly low, at an estimated 6,000
animals. (PO)

GALÁPAGOS FUR SEAL (*Arctocephalus galapagoensis*)

The endemic Galápagos fur seals are the smallest of the world's seven fur seal
species, with males only reaching 65–80kg in weight and females up to 27kg.
Despite their numbers (which approximate those of the sea lions) they are
less frequently seen by visitors than are sea lions. Their stronghold lies in the
upwelling zones in the west of the archipelago, away from most visitor sites.
The best place to see fur seals is at Puerto Egas on Santiago. Unlike sea lions,
fur seals rest in shady lava crevices and avoid body contact completely. They
have a very dense underfur (approximately 300,000 hairs per square inch),
growing between the longer, sparser, guard hairs. With large eyes and excellent
night vision, they are able to forage after dark, feeding on the deeper-water
lantern fishes (*Myctophidae*) which migrate upwards at night. They reproduce
mostly in the *garúa* season, producing on average only one pup every two years.
The pup has the longest suckling period of any pinniped, lasting two years or
more. As do sea lions, the male fur seal copulates on land within its territory
Males become territorial at nine years of age and usually remain dominant for
three successive years. Females come into oestrus only a few days after giving
birth, and are mated. Pups moult their baby coat to the adult pelage (fur) at
about five months. Six or seven months later they begin to feed independently
as well as suckling. Luckily, fur seals are not as susceptible to seal pox as the
sea lions, and their future looks bright. Seal pox is present but has not been
studied in the Galápagos and the effects are unknown.

WHALES AND DOLPHINS

There are approximately 76 species of cetaceans – whales, dolphins and porpoises – in the world, divided into two groups: those with teeth, and those with baleen. Eleven whales have baleen, the rest teeth. The baleen whales have a curtain of baleen plates (whalebone) which hangs from the upper jaw. Each plate has a hairy margin which acts as a sieve, trapping plankton. The baleen itself is made of keratin, the same substance as fingernails. When the whale takes a mouthful of water, its tongue acts like a piston, pushing the water out past the baleen sieve to trap food. Toothed whales hunt mostly fish, squid or meat, using a sophisticated echo-location technique to detect their prey.

Some whales can hold their breath for up to two hours, due to some very specialised adaptations. They are warm-blooded, and have a thick blubber layer to keep them warm in cold water. As mammals they nurse their young, called calves. Rather than the calf suckling, the female squirts milk into its mouth, using the muscles of her mammary glands. None of the whales in Galápagos are endemic, and many can be extremely difficult to identify. However, they are always a joy to watch.

TOOTHED WHALES (*Odontoceti*)

Probably the whales most often seen in Galápagos are the toothed whales, which range in size from the 45-ton bull sperm whale (*Physeter macrocephalus*) to the 75kg common dolphin (*Delphinus delphis*). One of the richest areas of Galápagos for all cetaceans is the Bolívar Channel and west of Fernandina. It is not unusual to see a pod of 40 or more sperm whales at rest on the surface, blowing and tail-lobbing, and sometimes submerging for 40 minutes or more, only to resurface invariably close to the point of descent. Sperm whales are the world's largest toothed animal. They descend to great depths (up to 3km) to feed principally on squid, including the little-known giant squid. Brownish in colour, they have wrinkled skin, with a dorsal fin that is no more than a shallow, triangular fleshy lump.

Of the medium-sized toothed whales, the most common are the short-finned pilot whales (*Globicephala macrorhyncus*), which are often seen around the central isles in groups of up to 20 or more individuals. They sometimes show curiosity and will approach small boats. False killer whales (*Pseudorca crassidens*) are similar, but do not have such a bulbous head.

Killer whales (*Orcinus orca*) (PO)

Occasionally false killers will approach boats and even ride on their bow-waves. Apart from fish, they attack dolphins and pinnipeds. Possibly the most dramatic whale of the Galápagos, however, is the orca or killer whale (*Orcinus orca*). The pandas of the sea with bold black-and-white markings, males reach 9.5m and weigh up to 8 tons. Orcas are highly predatory, feeding on pinnipeds, fish (including sharks) and even other whales. They are often seen very close to shore, either in groups of single males or in groups of one to 12 females and young, with one male. They are ubiquitous throughout the archipelago.

DOLPHINS

The Bolívar Channel and the colder waters of Fernandina and Isabela are excellent areas to encounter various dolphin species. Striped dolphins (*Stenella coeruleoalba*), common dolphins (*Delphinus delphis*) and possibly spinner dolphins (*Stenella longirostris*) are all commonly seen in the area. The latter are extremely difficult to identify out at sea. Sometimes dolphins collect in huge groups of several hundred individuals, acrobatically leaping clear of the water in play. They seldom approach a vessel, yet tolerate its presence. Perhaps the most commonly seen dolphin is the bottlenose dolphin (*Tursiops truncatus*), which is attracted to boats and regularly rides the bow-waves, even at night.

Bottlenose dolphins (*Tursiops truncatus*) are recognisable by their elongated nose or beak. (PO)

On such occasions, if there is any bioluminescent plankton (small organisms which give off light) their body shapes are outlined and illuminated in a beautiful ghostly green glow. They may appear any time, anywhere within the archipelago, usually in groups of one to 15 animals.

BALEEN WHALES (*Mysticeti*)

The most common baleen whales to be seen in the Galápagos are the humpback whale (*Megaptera novaeangliae*) and the Brydes whale (*Balaenoptera edeni*). Humpbacks are easily recognised, both for their jubilant acrobatics and for their unusual shape. Their most prominent features are their enormously long (5m) pectoral flippers. Brydes whales are one of the world's most tropical whales. They sometimes approach vessels and are even tolerant of snorkellers. Other baleen whales that may be spotted include the fin whale (*Balaenoptera physalus*), the sei whale (*Balaenoptera borealis*) and the minke whale (*Balaenoptera acutorostrata*).

LAND MAMMALS

O ceanic islands such as the Galápagos, which have never been attached to a mainland source of colonisation, tend to have few terrestrial mammals. There are six species of native mammals in the Galápagos: two species of rice rats, two species of bat, the fur seal and the sea lion. Obviously, the bats flew to the islands, while the fur seal and sea lion swam. Rats probably rafted on floating vegetation. Five or more species of endemic rats have become extinct since the arrival of man who, deliberately or otherwise, introduced the more competitive black rat (*Rattus rattus*), followed by the Norwegian rat (*Rattus norvegicus*).

RATS AND BATS

Until recently only two species of endemic rice rat were thought to exist: *Oryzomys bauri*, which lives on Santa Fé, and *Nesoryzomys narboroughii* on Fernandina. A third species, *Nesoryzomys fernandinae*, also lives on Fernandina, but was known only from bones found in owl pellets in 1979. However, in 1995 Robert Dowler saw a number of them, so their existence has been confirmed. Rice rats breed during the wet season, raising at least four young. They feed primarily on seeds and vegetable matter. In 1997 a group of scientists re-discovered a fourth species of the Santiago Island rice rat, *Nesoryzomys swarthy*, surprisingly co-existing with *Rattus rattus*.

Overlooked as often as the rice rats are the two native species of small insectivorous bats. The most common is the hoary bat (*Lasiurus cinereus*), which is also widespread throughout much of northern America. It is readily seen, particularly in Puerto Ayora, flitting around the streetlamps at night, feeding on the insects that gather there. By day, hoary bats roost secretively in dense, shady mangroves. The endemic subspecies *Lasiurus borealis brachyotis* is rarer, seldom seen and poorly understood. These two bats are best identified during handling; however, this is obviously not feasible except to researchers.

Being nocturnal, rice rats are seldom seen on Fernandina, although they can readily be spotted during the day on Sante Fé. This one is *Oryzomys bauri*. (PO)

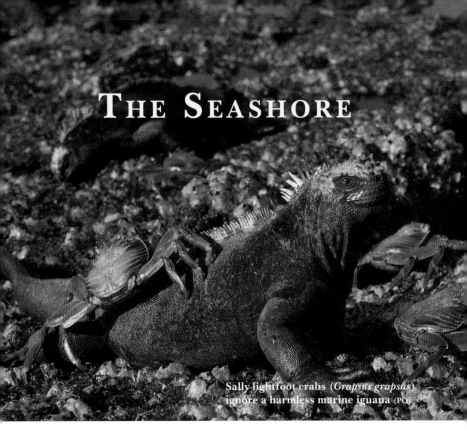

THE SEASHORE

Sally lightfoot crabs (*Grapsus grapsus*)
ignore a harmless marine iguana (PO)

O ne of the richest habitats in the islands is the narrow band where land
meets the cool ocean. Invertebrates mainly occupy the inter-tidal
zone. The most obvious crustacean is the sally lightfoot crab (*Grapsus
grapsus*), which commonly scavenges on wave-washed lava. The large adults with
flamboyant red, yellow and purple colouration are unmistakable. Young crabs
are dark and obscurely coloured to avoid predation.

On sandy shores ghost crabs (*Ocypode gaudichaudii*) can be seen. These
pale orange crabs spend much of their time searching in the sand for micro-
organisms, leaving tiny sand balls, or hiding in their burrows waiting to attack
other creatures. They get their name from the speed at which they disappear
into their holes. In mangrove swamps the fiddler crab (*Uca helleri*) is found in
large numbers.

Further inland you may see a snail shell 'walking': really a hermit crab
(*Coenobita compressa*) that has occupied an empty gastropod shell. These soft-
bodied squatters can only grow by finding a larger shell and 'moving house'.
Other crustaceans include the large acorn barnacle (*Megabalanus galapaganus*),
which can grow 2–5cm tall.

In tide pools, the only mollusc of note is the most primitive chiton (*Chiton
goodalli*), which has eight segmented, hard-shell plates. Chitons are oval
in shape and graze on algae. More apparent are sea urchins and sea stars
(echinoderms). They all have a five-fold internal structure. The pencil-spined

Above Sally lightfoot crab (*Grapsus grapsus*) These brightly coloured crabs, the scavengers of the coast, are unmistakable along the rocky shores. They will feast on anything they get their claws on, from sea lion placenta to other crustacea, including their own kind, and have an important role to play keeping the shores clear of organic detritus.

The name is thought to have originated from a Caribbean dancer and refers to their inherent agility jumping from rock to rock and climbing up vertical slopes. (PO)

Below Panamic cushion star (*Pentacerater cumingi*) Sea stars (often called starfish) are well represented in the Galápagos. They have radial symmetry, typically five 'arms' and a mouth on the underpart of the central, disc-shaped 'body'. They dwell on the sea bottom or in sub-tidal zones. As well as grazing on algae they predate on other creatures by everting their stomachs out of the body and absorbing the nutrients direct from the captive. (DH)

sea urchin (*Eucidaris thouarsii*) is dark brown, with short stubby spines that often get washed up on beaches. The green sea urchin (*Lytechinus semituberculatus*) is endemic. Its spines particularly adhere to human skin. Smooth sea urchins such as sand dollars (*Encope micropora*) can often be found as skeletons on beaches. Live sunstars (*Heliaster spp*) lurk under rocks in tide pools. These are like many-armed starfish. Whilst snorkelling you may see one of the giant sea stars, or the graphically named 'chocolate chip' sea star.

The marine iguana (*Amblyrhynchus cristatus*) is described under *Reptiles* (see page 45), but is an important part of the seashore habitat because it grazes on algae, particularly the sea lettuce (*Ulva lobata*).

Green sea urchin (*Lytechinus semituberculatus*) The green colour of this endemic sub-species of sea urchin comes from its delicate spines. Often washed up on beaches as part of the sand, or found browsing in tide pools, the urchins have the curious habit of picking up bits of shell or algae and carrying them around in what looks like a poor attempt at camouflage. Their numbers are greatly reduced by the prolonged warm water of El Niño events. (DH)

Galápagos penguin (*Spheniscus mendiculus*) chasing fish off Bartolomé Island. (PO)

UNDERWATER

Mexican or streamer hogfish (*Bodianus diplotaenia*) (PO)

Previous page Mexican or streamer hogfish (*Bodianus diplotaenia*) Like many members of the wrasse family (*Labridae*), males and females are quite different in maximum size as well as in shape and colour. This is a mature male, easy to spot with a distinct bump on the head and long tail 'streamers', absent on females and younger males. The very small juveniles are bright yellow with dark stripes and they often serve as cleaners, removing parasites from larger fishes. As the wrasse grow, the bright yellow fades to pale brown and the stripes become black. (JRG)

Above Shoal of yellow-tailed grunt (*Anisotremus interruptus*) (JRG)

Below King angelfish (*Holocanthus passer*) (JRG)

Over 400 species of fish have been recognised in the Galápagos, with 41 species unique to the islands (9.2% of the total, or approximately 23% of the shore fishes). The mixture of cool and tropical currents and different submarine habitats has created great diversity. Like the terrestrial fauna, many of the colourful reef fish are unafraid of humans. Scuba diving is becoming a popular activity among more adventurous visitors. However, because of strong currents and rapidly changing temperatures and visibility, it is not recommended for novice divers.

Jordan's snapper (*Lutjanus jordani*) with yellow-tailed grunt (*Anisotremus interruptus*) (JRG)

Bony Fishes

There is only space in a book of this nature to describe a few of the more common species and some rarer ones. There are other specialised guides to the marine life including *The Fishes of the Galápagos Islands* (see *Further Reading*, page 152).

ANGELFISH (*Pomacanthidae*)
The angelfish family is represented by two species in the Galápagos, but only one of them, the king or white-banded angelfish (*Holocanthus passer*), is common. This beautiful, disc-shaped fish has long, pointed fins, and is almost black with one vertical white bar. Angelfish usually swim in pairs or singly and are up to 30cm in length.

RED-LIPPED BATFISH (*Ogcocephalus darwinii*)
This endemic bottom-dwelling fish is probably the most curious. By day it 'walks' along the sea floor on flattened fins that act more as legs. At night it rises to the surface. It has a long snout and bright red lips; the rest of the body is brown on top, creamy white below. Elsewhere in the world, batfish are extremely wary, but here they will allow scuba divers to approach closely.

FOUR-EYED BLENNY (*Dialommus fuscus*)
Another curiosity, this tiny, dark-spotted tide-pool fish can see both above and below water as its eyes are split into two facets, each with different optics. It makes wriggling journeys up on the beach in search of small crabs and insects. Other adaptations enable it to breathe out of water for up to two hours!

Grey mickey or giant damselfish (*Microspathodon dorsalis*) (PO)

BUTTERFLYFISH
(*Chaetodontidae*)
Butterflyfish are oval and small, about 15cm long. They are distinguished from angelfish by their pointed, concave 'ski-jump' noses. Adults are usually yellow or silver, with dark stripes and yellow markings.

Rainbow wrasse (*Thalassoma lucasanum*) (PO)

DAMSELFISH
(*Pomacentridae*)
Damselfish are common in tide pools and reefs. Though diminutive, some are aggressive defenders of territory, and expend a lot of energy seeing off intruders. Each has its own patch of algae. Different species show distinctive markings when adult. The common yellow-tailed damsel (*Stegastes arcifrons*) has blue eyes and yellow lips, and grows to 6–15cm. The family includes the yellow and black-striped sergeant major (*Abudefduf troschelii*), a common reef fish.

PARROTFISH (*Scaridae*) and WRASSES (*Labridae*)
Parrotfish are so called because of their bright colours and powerful beak-like teeth. These common reef fishes come in a variety of shapes and colours. They are large elongated fish that reach about 45cm. Individuals may go through several colour phases and even changes of sex. Some have 'bumps' on the heads and others elongated fins or 'streamers'. Their strong teeth bite off lumps of coral, and grind them down to extract the algae. Parrotfish are important for recycling nutrients.

Wrasses (*Labridae*) are a related family and tend to be long and narrow. The rainbow wrasse (*Thalassoma lucasanum*) is like a tricolour flag, with blue, yellow and red hues.

PIPEFISH and SEA HORSES (*Syngathidae*)
These fish have elongated trumpet-shaped mouths. Pipefishes hide in crevices. Sea horses have protective external bony parts, prehensile tails and no fins. They swim in an upright position.

TRUMPETFISH (*Aulostomidae*)
Trumpetfish are long, slender fish, which have the ability to change colour. They often hunt in conjunction with larger fish, such as wrasse, and prefer regions of coral development.

PUFFERFISH (*Tetraodontidae*)

Being globe-shaped, pufferfish cannot move fast, but some species (*Diodontidae*) have defensive spines, and all are able to inflate themselves into an inedible ball by swallowing water or air. Sea lions sometimes play with them, but they are not good to eat, due to powerful toxins in the organs and skin. Pufferfish are a delicacy in Japan, where trained cooks carefully remove the edible flesh. They have sharp teeth to cope with a diet of molluscs and coral. The bullseye puffer, *Sphyroides annulatus*, is commonly seen around yachts, feeding on detritus.

The bulbous, odd-looking pufferfish have the ability to inflate themselves into a large ball to deter attackers. The guineafowl puffer (*Arothron meleagris*) is usually dark in colour with white spots; rare individuals are bright gold. They have strong teeth to crush invertebrates. Their skins and guts are highly poisonous. (PO)

REMORA (*Echeneis spp*)

Remora are oceanic hitch-hikers. They have a huge flat sucker on top of the head, with finely divided ridges that grip like a vice. They can attach themselves to dolphins, sharks, whales and even turtles. They clean their host of small parasites, and also eat scraps of leftovers.

SUNFISH (*Mola mola*)

Sunfish are related to puffers but look very different. At first sight, the sunfish resembles the giant head of a fish with a long dorsal fin, but no body behind. The fin can be distinguished from that of a shark because it moves slowly from side to side, not steadily forwards. These rare warm-water fish are all head, but can weigh up to a ton, and drift with the currents. They have a thick protective skin, and a small mouth with strong teeth for chewing jellyfish.

SURGEONFISH (*Acanthuridae*)

Surgeonfish are so named because they possess defensive 'scalpels' – sharp spines at the base of the tail, retracted into a sheath on each side. They are

Yellow-tailed surgeonfish (*Prionurus latclavius*) congregate in large schools. (PO)

sideways-flattened, oval-shaped fish. Yellow-tailed surgeonfish (*Prionurus latclavius*), grey with black stripes on the head, swim in large schools and are common on shallow reefs. Adults average 26cm in length.

TRIGGERFISH (Balistidae)
Triggerfish have a curious front spine which can be locked vertically by a second spine or 'trigger'. They are elliptical in profile, and vary from dark to brightly coloured. The fins undulate in waves as they swim.

SHARKS AND RAYS

Sharks and rays belong to the group of cartilaginous fish. Shark skins are rough because of their small, teeth-like scales. Some sharks have poor vision but can sense vibrations over a long distance; others have a good sense of smell. Several species of shark are found in the islands. Most are harmless to humans, but care should be taken to avoid swimming where fish blood is present, or near a feeding frenzy of boobies, pelicans or dolphins, as these attract hungry sharks.

Skates and rays are flattened and propel themselves using undulations of their extended pectoral fins. They have a graceful swimming motion, rather like 'flying'. Fifteen species, classified in seven different families, have been recorded from the islands.

BLACK-TIP SHARK (*Carcharhinus limbatus*)

Less common than the white-tip reef, and up to 2.5m long, this shark may be easily recognised by the black tips on all fins (except the upper tail) and its long, pointed snout. It is found near rocky reefs, alone or in small groups, but will usually swim away when approached by humans. Juveniles are commonly seen on the south beach of Bartolomé.

GALÁPAGOS SHARK (*Carcharhinus galapagoensis*)

These narrow sharks, silvery grey to brown, grow up to 2m. They are usually seen alone but sometimes in groups. They are active carnivores, found down to a depth of 100m and known to eat other sharks. Snorkellers will not encounter them but divers should keep a wary eye out for them.

Galápagos shark (*Carcharhinus galapagoensis*) (PO)

HAMMERHEAD SHARK (*Sphyrna lewini*)

This unmistakable shark has a flattened head that projects sideways, with eyes and nostrils to the sides (see photo below). The rest of the body is silvery grey and typically shark-like. Hammerheads grow up to 4m long. They hunt in packs and are common in the northern islands, but are not usually seen by snorkellers, and are not dangerous to divers unless fish blood is present.

Hammerhead sharks (*Sphyrna lewini*) have flattened heads which extend either side; the head of this species is 'scalloped' at the front. They are found mainly around the northern islands, either alone or in large schools. (JRG)

White-tip reef shark (*Triaendon obesus*) These are common throughout the archipelago, though thanks to the abundance of smaller fish are never a danger to humans. (PO)

A whale shark (*Rhincodon typus*) swimming with other tropical fish. (PO)

WHALE SHARK (*Rhincodon typus*)

Despite their huge size of up to 18m, these sharks are innocuous plankton-feeders. The world's largest fish, they are found throughout the tropical and temperate oceans. They follow upwelling currents rich in life, such as the Humboldt. Their huge mouths can swallow vast quantities of plankton.

Whale sharks are grey with yellowish white spots. Although they are not common, they may be seen on dive trips to the islands of Darwin and Wolf in the far northwest.

WHITE-TIP REEF SHARK (*Triaendon obesus*)

These classic pointed-nose sharks will grow to 2.13m, although individuals over 1.6m are rare. They are a silvery grey colour with white tips to their first dorsal fin and tail. The most common shark species, they are found around rocky reefs, under coral heads and in caves. They are docile sharks that feed at night, and are not thought to be dangerous, but take your guide's advice if diving.

GOLDEN RAY (*Rhinoptera steindachneri*)

These are small rays, about 75cm across the 'wings'. They swim in large schools in quiet lagoons. Their name comes from their yellow-coloured topside – they are also called 'mustard rays'. They have a blunt head with two lobes, and a long, whip-like tail.

MANTA RAY (*Manta hamiltoni*)

Manta rays are giant plankton-feeding creatures up to 7m across, though usually about 3m. They are dark on top but white below. The head is built around a huge mouth with movable side-lobes that help to scoop in food. Manta rays have a long, thin tail. They usually feed near the surface. Once called 'devil fishes' by old seafarers, these are harmless and graceful fish. Occasionally they 'leap' out of the ocean and land with a loud belly-flop; this may be an attempt to shake off parasites or remoras.

Spotted eagle ray (*Aetobatus narinari*) (PO)

SPOTTED EAGLE RAY (*Aetobatus narinari*)

There are two kinds of eagle ray in the Galápagos, but only the spotted form is common. These are beautiful rays whose top side is covered in white spots on a black background. Also known as 'leopard rays', they are white underneath. They have pointed heads and long, narrow tails with defensive spines, and are common in the mangrove lagoons such as Caleta Tortuga Negra. Usually small individuals 1m across are seen, but they can reach twice that size. These rays often swim in schools, and feed on crustaceans, molluscs and octopus.

STINGRAY (*Dasyatididae*)

Stingrays live on the sea floor and have long, narrow tails. The defensive sting is at the base of the tail, not the tip. Though they spend much time hidden just under the sand waiting for prey, they can swim well and chase at quite a speed! The stingray family includes the large, disc-shaped 'marbled' ray (*Taeniura meyeri*), which can grow up to 2m excluding the tail, and the more angular 'diamond' stingray (*Dasyatis brevis*).

The diamond stingray (*Dasyatis brevis*), like the shark, belongs to the group of cartilaginous fish. Rays have a flattened body disc which enables them to hide on the sea floor. To swim they wave these fins like 'wings'. The defensive sting lies at the base of the tail, not the tip. They are not aggressive when swimming but could inflict a nasty wound if stepped upon. (DH)

ISLAND LANDINGS
AND VISITOR SITES

Tourist yacht with marine iguana (JRG)

INFORMATION FOR VISITORS

Landings at the visitor sites are either 'Wet' (you get your feet wet landing on beaches) or 'Dry' (you land on rocks or at purpose-built docks). You must be steady on your feet to visit the islands and to get in and out of the dinghies. Some walks can be uneven and rocky, but the pace is usually very slow in order to observe the wildlife. A walking stick may be useful. Although distances are short, usually 2–5km, remember that it is very hot.

Clothing Shorts and T-shirts are the norm, but take a long-sleeved shirt and long trousers in case of sunburn. Sun hats and strong factor suncream are essential. Wear comfortable walking shoes or trainers, or sandals for beaches. A sweater or jacket may be needed for cooler evenings.

Equipment A daypack is useful. Suggested equipment includes small water bottle, swimsuit, sunglasses, insect repellent (in the wet season), camera (in plastic bag to keep dry), binoculars, notebook and pencils.

Diving and snorkelling The underwater world in Galápagos is as beguiling as that on land: with many unique species, the unusual sight of penguins and sea lions in the tropics, plenty of big creatures like turtles, sharks and rays and the steep walls of lava that disappear into the depths. Most boats give plenty of opportunity to snorkel and the equipment can be loaned or hired on board. On average there is at least one chance to snorkel every day, so it is worth preparing beforehand by practising in a pool. During the cool season (May–November) you may like to wear a wetsuit, and again many boats have these for rent, but do check with your operator beforehand. It is possible to swim throughout the year, but wear a T-shirt to avoid sunburn. Because of the variable currents, water temperature can vary from island to island. Snorkelling can be done from the shore for beginners or, for the more confident, from a dinghy (*panga*), where there is generally clearer water. Near shore you will see colourful reef fish like parrot- or angelfish, sea lions, turtles and small sharks (nothing to fear as they are well fed). The deeper 'blue' waters reveal schools of jacks, tuna, bigger turtles and rare hammerhead sharks.

The best snorkelling sites are: Bartolomé islet; Española: Gardner Bay, Gardner and Osborn islets; Floreana: Devil's Crown, Champion, and Endeby islets; Genovesa: Darwin Bay; Isabela: Tagus Cove, Tintoreras, Punta Vicente Roca; Rábida Island; San Cristóbal: Punta Pitt; Santa Cruz: Bachas Beach; Sombrero Chino.

The Galápagos are a world-class destination for scuba diving. At present it is not permitted to dive from regular natural history cruises, unless an arrangement has been made with a local dive shop to do this instead of some land visits. Serious divers can book on diving-only cruises with specialist operators. These will visit the two far-flung islands of Darwin and Wolf, which are challenging but rewarding dives, with huge schools of hammerhead sharks. If you are on a hotel-based holiday, day-trip diving can be arranged on Santa Cruz and San Cristóbal islands with local dive shops from whom all equipment can be hired.

 Particularly good location for snorkelling

SANTA CRUZ (INDEFATIGABLE ISLAND)

Santa Cruz is the most central of the islands, with the largest population of all the five inhabited ones. The town of Puerto Ayora has been the main base for tourism for the last 25 years, and is home to the national park headquarters and Charles Darwin Research Centre. The island has all the recognised vegetation zones, though much of the native flora has been destroyed by introduced plants and animals. The southeast is much wetter, for it faces the trade winds. Probably the highest number of bird species can be seen overall on Santa Cruz, including nine species of Darwin's finches and the rare Galápagos variety of Hawaiian or dark-rumped petrel.

The lava tubes

Travelling inland on the road to Baltra, just outside town on the left there is a large lava tube, about the size of a tunnel on the London underground; it is not advisable to go inside, as the roof looks unstable. The road leads up to the farming community of Bellavista. As you turn right and continue past the plaza, there are more lava tubes on a private farm; follow the signs to '*los tuneles*'. Another trail leads northeast out of the square to the highlands proper, within the boundaries of the national park and the *miconia* vegetation zone.

Bachas Beach

The name is Spanglish for 'barges', which were wrecked offshore during World War II. A common first landing site, there is a delightful swimming beach here, with a lagoon behind, and a longer beach for a stroll and wildlife-watching. The saltwater lagoon often has great blue herons and small waders such as sanderlings and semi-palmated plovers. Both beaches are nesting areas for green sea turtles, which leave tracks in the sand to the back of the beach, especially from November to February. A wet landing and open area on the beach mean one can explore at leisure. Marine iguanas lurk on the rocks between the beaches; hermit crabs create tiny tracks in the sand.

Caleta Tortuga Negra (Black Turtle Cove)

No landing is allowed at this tranquil lagoon. One enters by dinghy into a sheltered area surrounded by mangroves. Further in, motors are switched off and paddles are brought into silent action. The only sound is the occasional hiss of a turtle coming up for air. From December to March the Pacific green (not black) turtles come to breed here in peace and quiet. Young white-tip reef sharks are often seen, especially at the fast-flowing narrows between the main lagoon and the smaller inlets of water. Perhaps the most majestic sight of all is a school of dozens of spotted eagle rays or golden rays, gliding in unison. Three species of mangrove, red, white and black, are found at the edges of the lagoon. Herons and pelicans take advantage of the easy fishing here. It is a special place and very different from all other sites.

Black Turtle Cove is accessible only by dinghy. (DH)

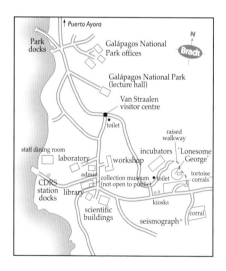

Charles Darwin Research Station (CDRS)

Though primarily an international scientific research station and not a tourist site, this is one of the most visited spots in the islands. It is situated just outside the town of Puerto Ayora and next to the Galápagos National Park offices, with which the CDRS is closely linked. If you land by sea you will arrive through mangroves, and see some of the biggest marine iguanas lazing on the dock. Arriving by road, there is a useful map of the station near the entrance. The first stop is the Van Straalen Hall, a visitor centre with self-explanatory wall panels about geology, climate, natural history and conservation. CDRS personnel give periodic talks about island ecology and how you can help by donating funds. The path continues to the old tortoise raising centre – which now has information about man's destruction of these reptiles – and on to the new tortoise incubators, where giant tortoises are hatched and raised until they can be safely returned to their island homes. A raised wooden walkway curves through the transitional zone vegetation and on to the corrals of fully grown tortoises. Most poignant of all is the enclosed section where 'Lonesome George', the sole survivor of the Pinta Island subspecies, now resides with some females from Volcán Wolf on Isabela. Despite all encouragement he has failed to take an interest in his companions! The CDRS is also a great place to spot finches and mockingbirds.

The Highlands – Media Luna and Cerro Crocker

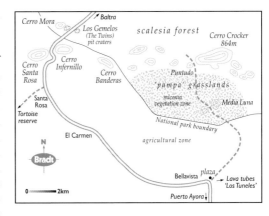

The trail starts in the Pampa or open area of pastures, with avocado groves and giant bamboo trees, then winds into dense *miconia* vegetation. Media Luna is one of several crescent-shaped eroded volcano cones, now covered in vegetation. The area has suffered from fires, cattle and introduced plants like guava. The rare Galápagos rail can be heard and occasionally seen. Take a rain jacket. It can get misty and muddy, and the trail is obscure. It is not advisable to hike alone in the highlands; go with a guide.

The summit of the island, Cerro Crocker, stands at 864m. Fit walkers will reach it 2½ hours after leaving Bellavista (round trip 14km). On a clear day the view is outstanding, with a 360° panorama over most of the archipelago. The Galápagos variety of the Hawaiian petrel nests in this region, but is rare due to the predations of dogs and rats.

Cerro Dragón (Dragon Hill)

From the landing at a crescent-shaped beach, the footpath climbs to an area frequented by land iguanas. These large, orange-yellow creatures were once part of the Darwin Station's breeding programme. Along the trail you may see Darwin's finches, and yellow warblers, and from the top of Dragon Hill is a majestic view of the bay. The path circles back down behind the beach; walk quietly here so as not to startle flamingos and other waders that feed in the brackish lagoon.

Two lesser-known sites nearby are **Conway Bay** and **Whale Bay**, both of which have similar colonies of land iguanas. Attacks by feral dogs have now been brought under control, and many captive-bred iguanas have been successfully repatriated.

The Tortoise Reserve

The reserve is now open to visitors, following a mystery virus that attacked the tortoises. It affords a chance to see giant tortoises in the wild, as opposed

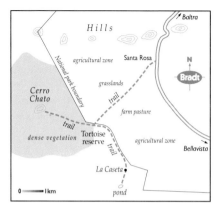

to easier trips to private farms. To reach the reserve, you take a long hike down from the village of Santa Rosa. The track goes through open pasture, where cows graze alongside tortoises, and you can often spot vermilion and broad-billed flycatchers. Other land birds include several species of Darwin's finch, the elusive Galápagos rail, cattle egrets, smooth-billed ani, dark-billed cuckoo and the ubiquitous yellow warbler.

The walk should not be undertaken lightly; go with a guide. It can be extremely hot, especially on the uphill return. Take plenty of water. It may be possible to hire horses in Santa Rosa; check at the park office. Good boots and waterproofs are essential, as the *garúa* mist can turn the path into a quagmire. It is about 3km to the reserve entrance, where there is a choice of trails: left to La Caseta and a pond (about another 2km), or right to Cerro Chato (another 3km). Both trails can be good for seeing tortoises among true native vegetation, but the forest can get so dense that spotting the reptiles is an acquired art. Endemic trees include the Galápagos guava or *guayabillo* (*Psidium galapageium*), the daisy tree (*Scalesia pedunculata*), and the sticky-fruited pega-pega (*Pisonia floribunda*).

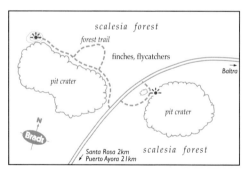

Los Gemelos (The Twins)

Highland tours and even the bus to Baltra usually stop at these two pit craters, which lie either side of the road beyond Santa Rosa. The Twins were empty magma chambers that collapsed in on themselves due to the weight of overlying rocks. Now these impressive round 'chasms' are clothed in vegetation; they are a good place to spot flycatchers and the elusive woodpecker finch. Near the road, native plants such as Darwin's daisy have sadly been taken over by introduced elephant grass, but the more robust *scalesia* trees are thriving. Keep an eye out for the short-eared owl perching in the vicinity.

Tortuga (Turtle) Bay

Turtle Bay is a beautiful, fine white-sand beach about an hour's walk from Puerto Ayora. There is now an easy marked path southeast of town, but the distance of

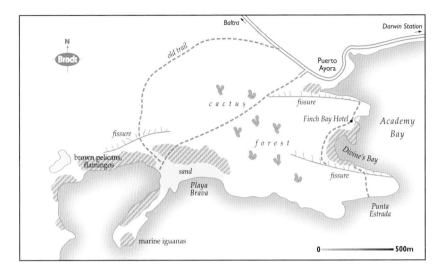

nearly 3km over lava has kept the beach from being over-exploited. There are no shops, so take some drink and snacks if you wish to spend time here.

A promontory divides the beach; the east side is exposed to wind and rolling waves (be careful of the undertow when swimming). Beyond is a quiet, protected lagoon surrounded by mangroves. Brown pelicans nest here in the warm season. Occasionally flamingos can be seen too. The sparse dunes behind the beach are protected by the endemic shrub *Nolana galapagoensis* and the purple-flowered beach morning glory vine. On the rocky point, marine iguanas can be observed, and out at sea sharks are not uncommon.

DAPHNE MAJOR

A real treat, Daphne is the most restricted visitor site. Only yachts with a maximum capacity of 12 passengers can visit once a month. The landing is only for fit people who can leap off a moving *panga* on to a near-vertical cliff covered in bird droppings.

Once ashore on this steep, eroded tuff cone, you feel like a castaway as your yacht disappears around the island. You have to step over the Nazca (masked) boobies who nest all over the narrow trail. It is a wonderful place to attempt the impossible, and photograph red-billed tropicbirds in flight. The nests are hidden in crevices along with the odd short-eared owl. Eventually the summit of the trail ends at a panoramic ledge with a view of two craters. Both contain hundreds of nesting blue-footed boobies, which mark their territories with a white ring of guano. How parent boobies recognise their patch is anyone's guess. The heat inside the craters reaches unbearable levels (tourists are not allowed down). Finally, as testament to the determination or madness of scientists, every single Darwin's finch on this island has been ringed and studied in intimate detail for more than two decades! Read Jonathan Weiner's study *The Beak of the Finch*.

ISLA MOSQUERA

A tiny reef of lava covered with coral sand, Mosquera lies between Baltra and Seymour; many boats pass by but few stop here. It is not an easy landing at low tide – you have to wade the last few metres over hidden boulders. Mosquera is inhabited by many sea lions, which are at home gliding into the tide pools. The lack of a marked trail gives a nice exploratory feeling to this visit. Among the sand are a few littoral plants like seaside heliotrope (*Heliotropium curassavicum*) and sea purslane (*Sesuvium*). Shore birds like sanderlings and semi-palmated plovers have an uncanny knack for dodging the surf.

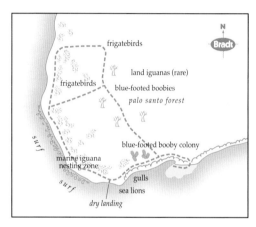

NORTH SEYMOUR

Situated next to Baltra, North Seymour is one of the most-visited islands. It is worth going ashore before breakfast in order to avoid the crowds. Even daytrip boats get here from Santa Cruz. The dry landing on black basaltic lava can be slippery, and is quite a test for the *panga* driver. After a short climb over the 'pillow lavas' formed by quick cooling underwater, the rest of the trail is flat and easy, apart from some boulders on the frigatebird loop. The landing is rich in wildlife: sea lions, swallow-tailed gulls, lava gulls, tropicbirds, brown noddy terns and pelicans. The trail is a large loop; you can either go clockwise along the shore or head inland to visit the booby colony first.

Heading along the shore, you traverse a wide expanse of sand criss-crossed with marine iguana trails. These reptiles nest here, so be careful where you tread. Some of the islands' finest waves pound a boulder beach on your left; young sea lions often body-surf here. Looking west, there are good views of the two Daphne islands, Major and Minor.

Right of the trail are saltbush clumps on which magnificent frigatebirds nest. If you are lucky you will see a male with his huge red balloon of throat pouch trying to impress a female. Competition is fierce, especially as great frigatebirds also get in on the act.

Both species nest in the trees; frigates are unusual for Galápagos seabirds in building a nest of twigs. A side trail goes inland to the breeding area. Here it can get a bit rocky, so watch your step. Another branch turns the other way to a flatter area where blue-footed boobies nest. During courtship they spend hours handing nesting materials (twigs and small stones) to each other, but never actually construct a nest. The area where the eggs are laid is marked by a

Frigatebirds nest close to the trail on North Seymour. (DH)

ring of white guano. Seymour is a good place to watch their theatrical courtship displays: the amusing 'dance of the blue-foots'.

The palo santo trees here are an endemic species, *Bursera malacophylla*, a dwarf variety of the aromatic tree. During the *garúa* season they look dead, but after the rains in February, they turn green almost overnight. Other endemic plants include *Opuntia* cactus, *Croton*, *Castela*, and *Sesuvium*. On rare occasions large land iguanas are seen under a shady bush. They were originally from Baltra (or South Seymour), but were brought over here by scientists many years ago to see if they would survive.

SANTA FÉ (BARRINGTON ISLAND) 🥾

The only visitor site on Santa Fé lies behind a pretty, sheltered bay in the northeast: a perfect anchorage and a good snorkelling spot. This small island is formed of uplifted, submarine basaltic lavas, formed around four million years ago. Much of it is a faulted plateau covered with a forest of giant *Opuntia* cacti.

The unnamed bay with a white sandy floor and turquoise waters is an impressive place to arrive. The shallow water means only small boats can visit. Along the natural harbour you can snorkel with young sea lions, but watch out for any big males – they have been known to attack humans here. Schools of yellow-tailed surgeonfish, sergeant majors, damsel- and parrotfish can be seen, plus the odd grouper, stingray and white-tip reef shark (these are harmless).

The wet landings on either beach can also be tricky, with the vigilant male sea lion 'beach masters' on the prowl! Ignore the guide's advice at your peril.

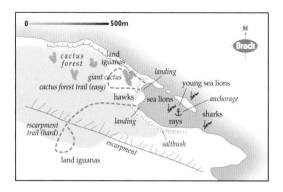

The beach has saltbush and *Maytenus* behind. There are two trails. The first is a tough walk along a dried watercourse, to a high escarpment to the southeast which is great for views (1.5km each way); the second is a short, fruitful loop that climbs through the arid vegetation to some giant *Opuntia* forest where land iguanas may be seen (800m). This second trail is the most commonly followed.

As you walk through the dense bushes on the short trail, watch out for the Croton bushes, an endemic plant with an indelible stain. The most spectacular plants are the giant prickly pear cacti (*Opuntia echios barringtonensis*), unique to Santa Fé. Listen carefully for rustling sounds; they could be made by the endemic rice rat, a big-eared rodent straight out of a Disney film. These are extremely rare; the only other island with endemic rodents is Fernandina. The Galápagos dove is common on the trail, as are painted locusts, often pursued by a snake or two. The park monument is often a vantage point to spy a Galápagos hawk. The highlight is the land iguana (*Conolophus pallidus*), a lighter-coloured iguana that is endemic to Santa Fé.

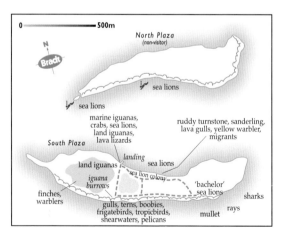

SOUTH PLAZA

Only the southernmost of the two Plaza islets is open to visitors. The pair lie a few hundred metres off the northeast coast of Santa Cruz, separated by a channel. Despite being only a kilometre long and little wider than 100m, South Plaza contains an amazing variety of life. Close to Baltra and Puerto Ayora, it is probably the most visited site of all, yet I once saw the nest of a lava gull, the rarest gull in the world.

The landing is dry; the park service having built a landing to accommodate the many visitors. The dock is often taken over by large male sea lions and their young, so before it is safe to land the guides have to shoo them away by clapping. Step carefully over the white guano and crab-covered rocks. As your eyes get used to the glare, you'll spot the land iguanas under the shadows of the *Opuntia*. These are one of the smallest subspecies of land iguanas. Early visitors used to feed them bananas, which may be one reason why they still congregate here. Their attraction to things yellow is more likely because of the tasty prickly pear flowers. The less colourful, younger individuals are often confused with marine iguanas, which can also be found happily walking right across the island. It is here that a hybrid of the two species has been recorded.

The trail heads up a gentle incline to a steep cliff. Like Seymour, Santa Fé and Española, geologically South Plaza is an uplifted piece of sea floor. The vegetation belongs to the arid and littoral zones: half the island is covered with saltbush (*Cryptocarpus pyriformis*), leatherleaf (*Maytenus*) and thorn scrub (*Scutia pauciflora*). The side with the trail is treeless, but covered with a rock garden-like mat of the endemic sea purslane whose succulent leaves turn red from May to December. The similar-looking *Portulaca howelli* (yellow flowers) is relished by the vegetarian land iguanas. This is a good place to get started on recognition of Darwin's finches; only the medium, small and cactus ground finches live here.

The cliff is surprisingly windy, and a great place for red-billed tropicbirds, swallow-tailed gulls, brown pelicans, and the odd frigatebird. Don't get too close to the edge; fatal accidents have occurred! It is easy to get engrossed in the mating habits of the gulls on the ledges. The trail snakes along the cliff edge for a few hundred metres. Offshore can be spotted Galápagos shearwaters, brown noddy terns and schools of mullet and surgeonfish. Farther out, dolphins, mantas and even killer whales have been seen.

The trail turns at a well-worn platform of polished lava, known as the 'bachelor sea lion colony': a motley collection of mainly elderly male sea lions who have lost their territories. Amazingly, they climb up the cliff via some rocky steps; it is the price they pay to get some peace and quiet. Many wear battle scars and shark bites.

Heading back down to the channel, the trail runs behind one of the most concentrated sea lion colonies in the islands. About 1,000 shift around as males continually vie for 'harems' of about 20 females. The pups are endearing and will often approach you, but you must not go up to them. Keep your eye out for migratory waders like sanderlings, knots, plovers and kelp gull.

Snorkelling off South Plaza is not allowed because of the number of sea lions. North Plaza is a good spot for experienced swimmers to cavort with juvenile sea lions, either within the channel or on the north side. Currents can be strong.

SAN CRISTÓBAL (CHATHAM ISLAND)
The airstrip here has opened up San Cristóbal to visitors, and the town of Puerto Baquerizo Moreno is growing fast. One positive addition has been the construction of a visitor interpretation centre.

Puerto Baquerizo Moreno

This is the official capital of the archipelago, situated in Wreck Bay to the southeast of San Cristóbal. Once a sleepy fishing port, it is now a booming tourist town as many of the yacht companies have switched their operations to commence from here. There are a few shops, hotels and restaurants along the waterfront, but the absence of a beach makes it worth getting out of the hot atmosphere to the surrounding coves. As you land at the dock the naval base is to the right side and the park offices to the left. A few hundred metres to the left is the Visitor Interpretation Centre, which has explanatory panels in English and Spanish; there are no refreshments or souvenirs available. Beyond the centre, it is worthwhile continuing to Frigatebird Hill for the views and birds. Day trips to El Junco Lagoon can be arranged from the port.

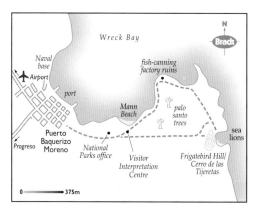

Frigatebird Hill (Cerro de las Tijeretas)

Just a short walk eastwards from Puerto Baquerizo Moreno is a hill where both species of frigatebird live. The hill drops off to a steep cliff, and a good view of the bay below makes the climb worthwhile. The round trip is 2km. You can cool off at the beach on the way back.

El Junco Lagoon

In the highlands of San Cristóbal lies the only freshwater lake in the archipelago, a rain-filled crater almost 300m across and 6m deep. The endemic variety of the Bahama or white-cheeked pintail ducks are at home here, together with common gallinules and resident migrants like the whimbrel and semi-palmated plover. Seven species of Darwin's finches have been recorded, though spotting them is not easy. At this altitude the air is pleasantly fresh, and the vegetation dense with introduced plants. You can see the endemic *miconia* and tree ferns, as well as some rare aquatic plants and sedges. A vehicle is required; a round trip usually takes about three hours.

Punta Pitt

In the extreme northeast of San Cristóbal, this site affords the chance to see all three species of booby. The landing is wet, on a green sand beach where you will receive the usual sea lion welcome. The trail climbs up the side of a steep tuff cliff, the slopes of an eroded volcanic cone; it's quite an energetic up-and-down trail, but the views will beckon you on. Frigates can be seen in the palo santo trees, whilst red-footed boobies prefer the *Cordia lutea* and smaller trees. Nazva (masked) boobies and blue-foots stake claims on the ground, with the masked variety closer to the cliff edge. The trail has a loop near the end where the succulent sea purslane makes a reddish mat in the dry season.

La Galapaguera

A short way west of Punta Pitt is a little-visited site where giant tortoises can sometimes be seen in the wild. The trail gets overgrown; take care and follow the guide.

Cerro Brujo

Some yachts embark here first in order to enjoy a subtle introduction to the Galápagos. There is a beautiful long, white, powder-sand beach, with pleasant swimming and snorkelling and good sea-kayaking opportunities. Sea lions, boobies and pelicans are found, but do not breed in large numbers.

Cerro Colorado Visitor Centre

On southeast San Cristóbal, a 40-minute journey by road from the port takes you to the Cerro Colorado Visitor Centre. This includes a large tortoise corral, an interpretation centre, conference room, gift shop, food bar, etc. The captive breeding centre includes a herpetology lab and tortoise growing pens with interpretive trails. The main purpose of the centre is to boost the population of the San Cristóbal tortoise (*Geochelone chatamensis*), which became extinct on much of the island due to the whalers and introduced animals. The tortoise station or Galapaguera has been designed to be as natural as possible. Along the trail you can see different species of native and endemic plants: cat's claw (*Zanthoxylum fagara*), poison apple (*Hippomane mancinella*), matazarno (*Piscidia carthagenensis*), needle-leaf daisy (*Macraea laricifolia*), sunflower tree (*Scalesia pedunculata*), Galápagos croton (*Croton scouleri*), acacia (*Acacia sp*) and Galápagos guaya (*Psidium galapageium*). You can also see birds like the San Cristóbal mockingbird, yellow warbler, small ground finch, small tree finch and Galápagos flycatcher.

Puerto Chino

A few kilometres from the Galapaguera the road ends at a quarry, and from here you can walk the 1.5km to the coast. The area consists of ravines which have been deeply eroded by rains down to the shore. There is a rare succulent plant to be found in the vicinity, Galápagos rock-purslane (*Calandrinia galápagosa*). This place is used as a recreational area by the inhabitants of the island. The main fauna are lizards and finches. Beware of the poison apple trees, their sap can cause a rash.

Playa Ochoa 🐾

Ochoa Beach lies west of San Cristóbal Island, approximately half an hour by boat from Puerto Baquerizo Moreno. The visiting area is restricted to the beach, where there are often sea lions, and ghost and hermit crabs are common. Nearby is a lagoon visited by migrating birds and shorebirds plus the magnificent frigatebird and endemic lava gull. It is one of the sites where you can see the San Cristóbal mockingbird (*Nesomimus melanotis*). One of the notable trees is the native hardwood matazarno (*Piscidia carthagenensis*), a species highly valued by locals for its toughness and longevity.

LEÓN DORMIDO (KICKER ROCK)

Northeast of Wreck Bay, many tour boats pass close to these tall rocks, said by the Spanish to resemble a sleeping lion. In reality they are an eroded tuff cone, whose sheer-sided cliffs, cut through the middle, are frequented by boobies (blue-footed and Nazca), frigatebirds and red-billed tropicbirds. A *panga* can pass through this narrow sea channel, and more macho captains will also sail yachts through, hoping a wave will not tilt the mast against the cliff!

ISLA LOBOS 🐾

On this small rocky islet, an hour's sail from San Cristóbal, blue-footed boobies nest among saltbush and palo santo trees. There is no shortage of sea lions (*lobo* is short for the Spanish name, 'sea wolf'). The candelabra cactus (*Jasminocereus thouarsii*) is common and the trail short (only 300m). The landing to this peaceful spot is dry.

ESPAÑOLA (HOOD ISLAND)

This isolated, southernmost island has one of the most spectacular visitor sites, with extensive nesting colonies of seabirds (including from March to December the waved albatross) plus dramatic cliff scenery and the famous blowhole. Española is thought to be formed of uplifted submarine lavas that were eroded flat. The cliffs on the southern side make an ideal take-off site for the huge albatross. A high number of species are unique to Española Island (examples include the marine iguana, the mockingbird and the lava lizard), while it is also a good place to spot finches, including the large cactus finch and the warbler finch. The two visitor sites could not be more different: one is a rocky walk frequented by breeding seabirds, the other is a long, white, sandy beach where the best spots are usually taken by sea lions.

Punta Suárez

From the moment the dinghy heads towards the rocky point, you will be spellbound by the young sea lions surfing, and a reception committee of their parents barking on the tiny beach (a wet landing). A promontory of wave-rounded boulders protects the landing from some of the biggest waves in the archipelago. Large marine iguanas lie motionless like sentinels upon the rocks

– here more colourful than elsewhere, with hues of red and green. The circular trail is one of the longest, at about 4km.

A water bottle is a good idea. First you walk south through dense saltbush, then on a plateau of scrub (*Atriplex, Lycium, Grabowskia* and *Cacabus*). The trail continues on through a colony of masked boobies at the western edge of the island. Nazca (masked) boobies like the outer edges of islands, while the blue-foots prefer inland. The trail dips down to an eroded pebble beach; tread carefully as marine iguanas

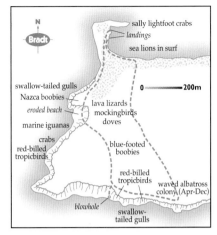

nest here! A pair of oystercatchers can usually be heard as you step into their domain. All along the coast the distinctive red-billed tropicbirds utter their screeching alarm calls; if you are lucky you will spot them entering the cave where they nest.

The trail heads inland through dancing blue-footed boobies, often oblivious to tourist legs at which they may make a half-hearted peck. The boobies keep a watchful eye out for the Galápagos hawk, which will pick off any chicks left unguarded, as will the snakes that slither between the boulders. The lava lizards are bigger here than on other islands, especially the black-spotted males. The mockingbirds also differ, with longer bills and aggressive behaviour (they untie tourists shoelaces or perch on their hats).

There is a good vantage point at the clifftop near the blowhole. Here you can contemplate the power of the sea, a vapour spout shoots up to 25m through a gap in the rock. A side trail drops through a crack to the place where the spray periodically shoots into the air. The trail now hugs the southern clifftops, and leads over boulders; watch your step! At the turning point of the trail from April to December, the waved albatross takes a run up to the cliff and launches into the abyss. Heading back inland, you reach the breeding area for albatross, whose theatrical displays are often the most memorable part of the trip. In the bushes keep an eye out for Española's three Darwin's finches: the large cactus, small ground, and tiny warbler finch. On the ground the pretty Galápagos dove forages, hardly ever flying. Getting back on the dinghy usually involves running the gauntlet of bull sea lions. Offshore, Galápagos shearwaters and storm petrels accompany you back to the boat.

Gardner Bay

Gardner Bay is one of the longest beaches in the Galápagos (2km). Its white coral sand is dazzling; sunglasses and a hat are a must, and shoes are needed

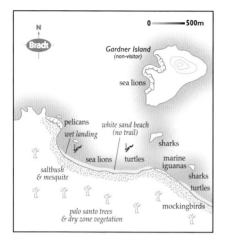

to stop the sand burning your feet! The landing is wet and there is no trail – the beach is an open area – you can stroll without being in a group. At first sight the beach does not appear to have much living on it, but what look like boulders are actually sleeping sea lions or an exhausted turtle that has laid her eggs. Behind the beach are palo verde (*Parkinsonia*), acacia (*Acacia sp*) and mesquite (*Prosopis*) as well as the common saltbush (*Cryptocarpus pyriformis*). You can spot the island's three finches here, plus mockingbirds, the rarer Galápagos martin and, playing along the surf, small wading birds such as sanderlings and the elegant wandering tattler. The rocks in the middle of the beach are great for marine iguanas and crabs. The coast beyond is for scientific use only. Though snorkelling off the beach sands is not good, the islets in the bay are excellent, with schools of yellow-tailed surgeonfish and the odd white-tip reef shark.

FLOREANA (CHARLES ISLAND)

Floreana is no longer an active volcanic island. Its uneven profile comes from long-extinct eruptions and parasitic cones now covered in palo santo forest. As the first island to be inhabited by humans, it has many introduced species, but tortoises are extinct as a result. Today there are only a handful of inhabitants, but many stories are told of the island's mysterious past (see *Death in Eden* box, page 6). The highlands are rarely visited by tourists, but are the only place to find the medium tree finch. The islets off the coast of Floreana such as Champion and Enderby are the only places where the Charles Island mockingbirds exist – they have been wiped out by cats on the main island.

Punta Cormorant

Punta Cormorant is a misnomer – there are no cormorants on Floreana; the name came from a US military vessel. However, there are many flamingos here. The landing on the beach is wet. The sand has a greenish tinge due to the large amount of a volcanic mineral called olivine. Often, green, pencil and white sea urchins are stranded on the beach, and there are shells for young sea lions to play with. A short trail begins by the big black and button mangrove trees towards the lagoon behind. The littoral vegetation is noteworthy because of two plants unique to this part of Floreana: the cutleaf daisy (*Lecocarpus pinnatifidus*), and a species of daisy tree (*Scalesia villosa*), with its hairy leaves and stems.

The endemic subspecies of passion flower (*Passiflora foetida*) is also found here.

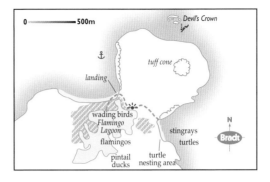

The large, brackish lagoon holds one of the biggest populations of flamingos in Galápagos. If you are quiet you may find one approaches within 5m of you. Flamingo nests are found on the far side of the lagoon; they look like mud pies. The adults parade around like regimental soldiers. Using binoculars you can find other waders, including black-necked stilts, whimbrels, willets, ruddy turnstones and phalaropes.

A longer trail goes around the east side of the lagoon. About halfway is a viewpoint on an old cinder cone. The vegetation is diverse, encompassing arid plants such as acacia, *Croton*, palo verde (*Parkinsonia*), mesquite (*Prosopis juliflora*), bitterbush (*Castela*), and transition zone trees: palo santo (*Bursera*), pearl berry (*Vallesia glabra*) and velvet shrub (*Waltheria ovata*). The trail crosses the point at its narrowest section and we are back into a fine sand dune with littoral plants: seaside heliotope, clubleaf (*Nolana galapagoensis*) and inkberry (*Scaevola plumieri*). The endemic Galápagos fritillary butterfly has also been seen here.

The 'flour' sand beach is a delightful spot to relax, but swimming is forbidden now because of the turtles and rays that frequent it. Ghost crabs scuttle over the intertidal zone. Turtles nest here from December to March. Novice snorkellers can practise back on the main beach where the sea lions are fairly quiet. For those with experience, a better place is the nearby islet of **Devil's Crown** (Onslow Island) 🐾. This sunken cinder cone has been filled by the sea, so the water is shallow inside but steep and deep outside. Corals abound with reef fishes such as parrotfish. Larger fish such as palometas school outside the crater. Underwater caves link the two, but beware of strong currents if you attempt to free-dive through them, and you might also meet a hammerhead *en route*!

Post Office Bay
This is a small bay a short sail west of Punta Cormorant. It is mainly of historical interest. The beach is a wet landing. The trail is only a few metres, but use sandals because of the sharp seeds of puncture vine (*Tribulus*).

In 1793, British navigators placed a large wooden barrel here, to leave messages and mail for homebound voyagers. A decade later it was used for espionage during the Anglo-American naval war. The tradition has continued until the present day, using replaced barrels over time, and it is now a way

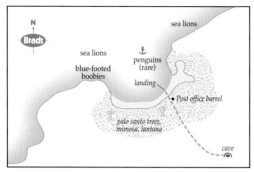

of sending postcards home. Visiting yachts have added their calling cards, pieces of carved driftwood, a practice which is accepted unofficially by the park. Beyond the barrel, a trail continues past the remains of an aborted Norwegian fish-canning enterprise. The walk continues to a lava tube that has been explored by cavers and descends to sea level. The skeletons of trapped sea turtles add to the gloom within.

Farther west is the small village community of Black Beach; here you can get cards printed with a Galápagos postmark at the Wittmer family guesthouse. The Wittmers were one of the first families to colonise the islands (see page 6).

Mirador de la Baronesa

The Mirador de la Baronesa is situated on the north coast of Floreana between the two more visited sites of Post Office Bay and Punta Cormorant. Apart from a beautiful stretch of coastline, which makes a great dinghy ride, this site is of historical significance, being named after the flamboyant Baroness Eloisa Von Wagner Bosquet. She was one of the pioneering inhabitants of the 1930s, and mysteriously disappeared after causing quite a stir with the other German settlers. She used this old cinder cone as a place to keep an eye out for passing yachts. Behind the beach where you land are the remains of a house built out of blocks of lava. The beach is used as a nesting place for marine turtles and is fringed by red mangrove bushes.

La Loberia

La Loberia means 'place of sea lions', though in Spanish they say 'sea-wolf'. On other islands there are similarly named places. This site is quite close to the village of Velasco Ibarra, the only port on Floreana. The trail is just under a kilometre long over sand and rocks. The main point of interest is the colony of sea lions. There are also marine iguanas on the rocks, and turtles can be seen in the shallow waters of the bays and inlets. This is also a good place to spot finches.

Highlands
The **Asilo de la Paz** (Haven of Peace) is worth the 8km bumpy road journey above the agricultural highlands to a hill draped in native *Scalesia pedunculata* forest where it is pleasantly cool. The trail is quite a steep trek and can be muddy after the rainy season. You will pass by a large rock corral with giant tortoises brought over from San Cristóbal (as they are extinct on Floreana). In the rocks at the top

In the highlands of Floreana, the slopes of Asilo de la Paz are covered in *Scalesia* forest. (DH)

of the trail is the main freshwater spring of the island, and some caves which were reputedly inhabited by early settler Patrick Watkins, later by Dr Ritter and his companion Dora Strauch and then the Wittmer family, until they built a proper house. A mysterious stone head was probably carved by the Wittmers. Birdwatchers should keep an eye out for the medium tree finch (*Camarhynchus pauper*) which is found only on this island. In these highlands nest the rare Galápagos petrel or *pata pegada* (*Pterodroma phaeopygia*). On the way down you can observe the introduced orchards of citrus fruit plums and tamarind. Lower down there is another trail to **Cerro Allieri**, a shallow cinder cone now covered in dense vegetation including an endemic rarity *Linux cratericota*.

SANTIAGO (JAMES ISLAND)

Lying almost central within the archipelago, Santiago is on most itineraries. As well as sites on both east and west, there are several small islets worth visiting nearby such as Sombrero Chino, Rábida and Bartolomé. Darwin himself was an early visitor to Santiago. Though man's impact has been heavy, with introduced goats, pigs, rats and donkeys evident and putting the tortoises at risk, there are still plenty of worthwhile sights, including the lava flow at Sullivan Bay and the fur seal grottos and tide pools near Puerto Egas (South James Bay). Here, after the rains, the vegetation is abundant with plenty of flowers, insects and land birds. With evidence of human activity, the island is now considered of 'archaeological' interest, especially Buccaneer Cove.

Buccaneer Cove

Few boats land here now, but during the 17th and 18th centuries this was an important site for sailors to careen (haul and clean) their ships, hunt for meat

Buccaneer Cove, Santiago (DH)

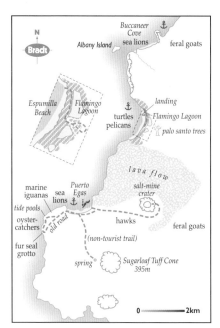

and collect firewood and water. The high tuff cliffs to the south of the bay are an impressive sight, whilst the contorted cinder to the north has been eroded into many shapes, including the famous 'Elephant' and 'Monk'. The beach is well populated with sea lions.

Espumilla Beach

Espumilla is a long, golden, sandy beach with a mangrove backdrop. It can be a tricky wet landing due to the breakers. Marine turtles nest here, ghost crabs keep the beach free of intruders, and wading birds dodge the surf. Behind are saline lagoons, once an important flamingo site, but after floods in 1983 the flamingos went elsewhere. Feral pigs have decimated the turtles' breeding chances. A short trail goes up into the vegetation of the transitional zone. This is a good place to spot some of the ten species of finch found on Santiago, and the vermilion and broad-billed flycatchers.

Puerto Egas (South James Bay)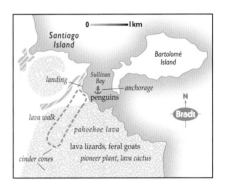

At first sight this landing seems forlorn, with odd bits of human detritus scattered around. The area was the site of two doomed salt-mining enterprises in the 1920s and 1960s. The park has decided to leave them as 'industrial archaeology'. Miners dug salt out of a crater to the east (today's residents are flamingos). Around the south of the bay, eroded tuff cliffs make interesting wave-cut shapes.

The tide pools beyond the point are a pleasant surprise. The trail is an open area between the old road and the sea. Large marine iguanas and sally lightfoot crabs abound. Brittlestars cling under rocks in the pools, and urchins and sea snails hide among anemones. Sea lettuce, food for iguanas, makes a green carpet over the black rock. Moray eels slither out of crevices in the pools; octopus keep a wary eye on you. A resident pair of oystercatchers tend their young. At the end of the trail, the large fissures that open to the sea are known as the fur seal grottoes; in these enchanting natural pools both species of sea lion rest and play. Coming back to earth, you reach every guide's favourite lava tube, called 'Darwin's Toilet', a cave that is periodically flushed by the action of the sea.

Sullivan Bay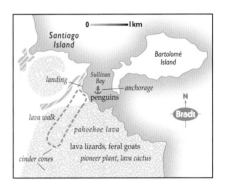

The bay is named after HMS *Beagle*'s second lieutenant, Bartholomew Sulivan (spelt with one 'l' – modern usage has changed this to two). This visitor site gives a chance to walk over a recent, barren, lava flow. The tiny coral sand beach provides a wet landing, or a dry one on the rocks nearby. The whole circuit is just under 2km. It can be quite hot, so a water bottle may come in handy.

The black, basaltic pahoehoe or ropey lava is about 100 years old, but looks as if it only just cooled. The lava has cooled into shapes reminiscent of ropes or intestines, or the ripples on a pond. It flowed gently around the cones of more explosive eruptions; they are much redder and are full of gas bubbles. The lava has cracked revealing layers of several flows. If you look carefully, you can find moulds of trees that were vaporised by the lava. Today, the only plants here are the tiny *Mollugo* carpetweed herb, and the rare lava cactus (*Brachycereus*). At the edges can be found volcanic glass or obsidian that crystallised rapidly.

BARTOLOMÉ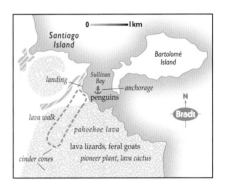

The panoramic view from the summit of Bartolomé is probably the most photographed landscape in the islands (see photo on page 7). Situated in Sullivan Bay off eastern Santiago, the island is geologically young and some of

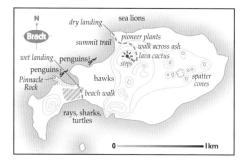

the 'spatter' or cinder cones look as if they were formed yesterday. A good snorkelling place lies at the foot of the Pinnacle Rock that leans into the bay. The cliff is an eroded tuff cone. A small family of Galápagos penguins lives in the shadows of the Pinnacle, and surprise bemused swimmers as they 'fly' through the waters of the bay. A dinghy ride is usually taken to locate the penguins.

Bartolomé is one of the most photogenic islands, with a variety of volcanic formations. (JRG)

The beach landing is wet. Unfortunately, the mangroves behind are a fly and mosquito breeding-ground, and horseflies love wet human legs. Take some repellent. A short ten-minute walk across a sand dune takes you to the southern beach, where harmless black-tip sharks and rays are often seen in the warm, shallow water. Snorkelling is banned here to protect the marine life. Ghost crabs creep over the sand and disappear as you approach. Look up at the sky and often you may see a juvenile Galápagos hawk hovering overhead. From January to March marine turtles come ashore to nest in the sand.

The summit trail begins with a dry landing, though sea lions make the purpose-built dock more exciting. The trail is a dusty walk through volcanic ash. The only vegetation is the 'pioneer plants', grey *Tiquilia* and greenish *Chamaesyce*. These are vital in binding the ash that fans down from the hill. The park wardens have built wooden steps up the hill to prevent further erosion by humans. The reddish spatter cones were minor eruptions of highly viscous material that cooled rapidly. The summit is such a cone; it seems higher than 114m as you climb the steps. The eastern side has many small lava tubes. The hike is better before 10.00 or after 16.00, when the light is softer. If you look carefully you can make out sunken craters in the sea below. In the distance you can see most of the central islands, the peaks of Isabela to the west, and on a clear day Marchena and Pinta to the north.

GENOVESA (TOWER ISLAND)

It is a long sail up to Genovesa, but worthwhile. The English name Tower refers to an admiral, not the shape of the island; it is a low, flat, isolated island with a huge sunken crater, into which you sail. The caldera walls form cliffs of about 25m above sea level but plunge down over 60m below the water. Genovesa is home to the biggest colony of red-footed boobies in Galápagos, and many great frigatebirds.

Darwin Bay

The wet landing is on a sharp white-coral sand beach (wear sandals or sneakers). The cliffs to the right, and the small lagoons behind, give the impression of a rock garden. Yellow-crowned night herons wait in the rocks, whilst white-cheeked pintail ducks occupy the lagoon. Galápagos doves go about their business on the ground, and lava gulls laugh at each other.

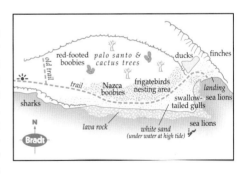

Walking westward along the sand, you come across a fissured ridge of lava through which the sea filters. At high tide much of the trail is underwater, and you have to wade a few metres. Swallow-tailed gulls favour this ridge to bring up their chicks; they warn off any visitors who get too close. On the other side of the trail great frigatebirds nest on the saltbush, sharing the bushes with red-footed boobies.

The trail continues above the high-tide level to a viewpoint over the bay. In the palo santo, cactus and *Croton* bushes can be found three species of Darwin's finches: the large ground, sharp-beaked and warbler finches. There are surprisingly no lava lizards, and the marine iguanas are the smallest in the archipelago.

Snorkelling along the rocks either side of the beach can be exciting, with strong surf but poor visibility. Sharks are not uncommon here.

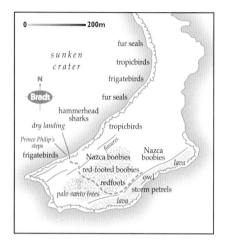

Prince Philip's Steps (El Barranco)

The long dinghy ride around the bay to the other side of Genovesa is one of the few chances to spot the reclusive fur seals in the crevices. Red-billed tropicbirds screech overhead with the greedy frigatebirds in pursuit. The landing is dry, but involves a scramble up 25m of rock. The 'steps', named after the Duke of Edinburgh, a visitor in 1965, are a natural rockfall, not purpose-built stairs as the name suggests.

Once on the top, the trail is flat, though uneven in places; the fragile plates of lava make a clunking sound as you walk over them. The trail is about 2km, and there is plenty to see. Nazca (masked) boobies nest just inland from the steps; then as you traverse a deep crevasse in the lava, you'll find red-footed boobies in the denser vegetation. The palo santo and muyuyo forest abruptly cease at a ridge of lava which flowed out from an impressive fissure below. Beyond that is an area of broken lava where clouds of storm petrels swarm mysteriously. After pondering the petrels' flight behaviour, you return the same way you came. Short-eared owls are common here but it takes a good eye to spot one as they are so well camouflaged. The lava cactus (*Brachycereus*) is easier to find. Standing at the end of the trail looking out to sea, you really feel you are on the edge of the archipelago.

RÁBIDA (JERVIS ISLAND)

The bright red beach (a wet landing) is made of sand eroded from cinder cliffs to the west. The beach is backed by saltbush (*Cryptocarpus pyriformis*), which hides a saltwater lagoon surrounded by black and white mangrove trees. Visitors usually walk first along the beach, as pelicans sometimes nest there on the saltbush. Young brown pelicans can be seen plunge-diving in the sea, looking clumsy alongside groups of blue-footed boobies.

In the lagoon white-cheeked pintail ducks and black-necked stilts are found. Flamingos have been known to breed here too, but recent increases in sea lion populations have seen them off. Young sea lions are happy as sandboys, but the big adult males get into scraps that can become bloody. Galápagos hawks occasionally hang around in the taller trees.

The interior of the island climbs to a single peak of an eroded cone, sparsely vegetated with palo santo, *Opuntia* cactus, *Croton scouleri*, and *Maytenus*. A trail loops around the point that lies east of the beach. It goes up steeply to a good

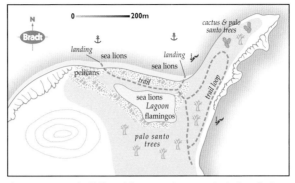

vantage point, then south to some red cliffs, with tempting snorkel sites below. The trail returns through the neatly spaced palo santo forest. There are nine species of Darwin's finches on Rábida. Feral goats have been eradicated by the park wardens.

Back on the beach, the rocks to the east make a perfect place to learn to snorkel. Schools of reef fish like damsels, surgeons, triggers and larger groupers and pufferfish make this an attractive place to plunge beneath the waves. There is little current as long as you do not swim out beyond the point. You may even see a pelican fishing underwater.

SOMBRERO CHINO (CHINESE HAT)

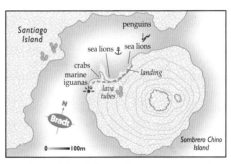

Only visited by the smallest yachts, Sombrero Chino is a beguiling site, a microcosm of Galápagos that lies just a couple of hundred metres off the southeast coast of Santiago. The islet is approached by a turquoise-coloured channel, one of the most picturesque anchorages in the archipelago. The whole island is a cinder cone with a steep-sided crown like a Chinese hat, hence the name. The sides are punctuated by minor spatter cones, lava tubes and patches of pahoehoe lava. Since these formations are extremely fragile, the trail is just a short one along the coast.

Littoral zone plants are found near the beach: saltbush *Cryptocarpus*, *Heliotopium*, *Portulaca howelli* and *Sesuvium edmunstonei*; the rest of the island is barren apart from sparse lava cactus (*Brachycereus*). Sea lion cubs are left in a nursery by the beach, and a solitary male 'beach master' keeps guard. Bright orange sally lightfoot crabs congregate on the dark rocks at the edge where the trail begins. The trail is only 350m each way to a peaceful but spray-soaked cliff looking out to sea, where marine iguanas are likely to be your only company.

The channel is a good snorkelling site, but there is less current on the far side off Santiago. Penguins can be found here. In the deeper parts of the channel there may also be manta rays and white-tip sharks.

ISABELA (ALBEMARLE ISLAND)

Isabela is the largest of all the islands, over 130km from north to south. It has five of the biggest volcanoes, including Volcán Wolf, which is the highest of all at 1,646m.

There are numerous smaller cones. The most notable is Volcán Ecuador, sliced in half by wave action; quite a sight to sail past. Despite its size much of Isabela is barren lava, with few places to disembark. We shall only describe the most visited landings. There have been recent eruptions on Cerro Azul, Sierra Negra and Wolf. Volcán Alcedo has the largest tortoise population and is the only one that visitors are allowed to climb. (Access is restricted at the time of writing because the park wardens are trying to eliminate feral goats.)

Volcán Alcedo

The wet landing at Alcedo is on to a small beach with coarse, black lava sand. The 20km round trip, which can be extended by a further 12km at the top of the rim to the south to get to the best tortoise area, is strenuous. Wear good hiking boots, leaving wet shoes high up on the beach. Take plenty of water, sunscreen and a hat as there is limited shade; plasters (Bandaids) may also be useful. Disembark as early as you are allowed; it is best to arrive at about 05.00, completing the hike by 16.00. Alternatively, you can arrange with the park authorities or your tour company to camp overnight at the rim, giving more time to explore the crater.

The first half of the climb is long, monotonous, and continuously uphill, so take several rest stops. About halfway up is a good shade and rest area under a prominent muyuyo tree; it is here that you may see the first of a few tortoises. The next part of the walk is a very steep and quite tough climb to the top, often on loose gravel or sand. It is easy to get lost. Always stay with your guide and in a group; if there are two guides, ask one to bring up the rear.

In addition to the tortoises, this hike also affords opportunities to see vermilion flycatchers, hawks, carpenter bees and several endemic plants. There are usually plenty of goats and donkeys on the way up and many more once you reach the rim. At the end of the walk, once back on the beach, look for land iguanas. (Note that this trail is closed at present.)

Punta Albemarle

As this is at the extreme north of Isabela, landings can sometimes be tricky during the hot season when the wind is coming from the north. This site is named after the Duke of Albemarle (the island was previously named Albemarle by the English sailors). The coastal area is ideal for dinghy rides among the coves and creeks formed by lava flows that reached the sea. The lava is of the ropey pahoehoe lava type. The area is fringed by mangroves. Some of the biggest marine iguanas in the archipelago are found here, and with a bit of luck you can see them feeding on seaweed. You can also observe the endemic flightless cormorant and other sea birds such as the endemic gulls. The site also has historical significance as it was the site of a US radar base during World War II.

Elizabeth Bay

The narrowest part of Isabela is called the Perry Isthmus. On its western side is a marine site (no landing) known as Elizabeth Bay. Yachts anchor a long way out near the islets of Marielas. The panga can take at least 20 minutes to reach the coast. On the way Galápagos shearwaters, brown noddy terns and blue-

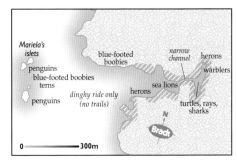

footed boobies can be seen. Along the rocks boobies rest, and marine iguanas congregate. Flightless cormorants are less common.

Your dinghy will enter a narrow channel flanked by mangroves, where great blue herons and lava herons fish. The *panga* driver will switch off the engine and paddle as the lagoon opens out. The occasional head of a sea turtle pops up for breath. Farther in are the biggest red and white mangroves in Galápagos. Amazingly, young sea lions come right inside the lagoon and have an unusual penchant for climbing the trees! The quiet waters are a refuge for schools of golden rays, spotted eagle rays and baby sharks. Around the islets in the bay can be a good place for penguins. It's is not easy to take pictures of black birds on dark rocks from a bobbing boat, but it is good fun trying. Tropicbirds screech overhead as if to mock.

Punta Moreno

This is one of the least-visited sites, due to its inaccessibility; the boatman needs some expertise to find the way in through a maze of mangrove lagoons. Basaltic pahoehoe and plate lava seems to stretch to the horizon. Wild dogs are at home here, living in packs, and the dry landing on what looks like virgin lava makes you feel as if you are the first humans to land.

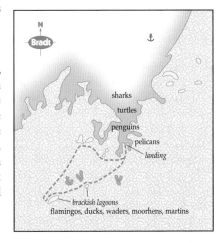

A semblance of a trail has been marked, the full circuit taking a couple of hours. Apart from the lava itself, the attractions are a series of brackish lagoons that appear in the black lava, like oases. These water-filled depressions are surprisingly full of life. The reeds around the edges are rich in insect life such as dragonflies, a rarity in Galápagos. Common gallinules or moorhens breed here, as do white-cheeked pintail ducks. Pelicans breed in the mangroves. Strangest of all are the flamingos, which one can approach more closely in Galápagos than elsewhere in the wild. Other birds, including egrets, herons, martins, sandpipers and semi-palmated plovers, can also be seen by the patient observer. On the lava itself, only lizards, painted locusts and the fragile plant Mollugo break the monotony. The endemic lava cactus and occasional candelabra cacti look like distant scarecrows.

Although snorkelling is not ideal from the landing as visibility is poor, a quick cool-off in the coastal pools is very welcome.

Tagus Cove

The steep-sided cove, named after a British warship that came here in 1814, is an impressive natural harbour. Early mariners carved their ships' names on the rocks; later, the custom degenerated into painted graffiti. (Now forbidden by the park authorities, it has been hard to stamp out.)

The landing is dry but can be tricky in a swell. The trail curves up a steep gully, and is strong on scenery, historic ambience and flora. Some of the oldest graffiti is carved in the tuff here, dating back to 1836 – the time of Darwin – though not by 'Chas' himself. Higher up, wooden steps have been built to prevent erosion. Nearby is a marked cross monument in memory of a young sailor who was lost at sea in the 20th century. The view improves the higher you get. Eventually the circular crater of Darwin's Lake appears below. The story goes that the naturalist ran down and took a large gulp, expecting it to be fresh water, only to find to his disgust that it was briny.

The trail half circles the ridge of the crater. Many native plants are to be found, including muyuyo (*Cordia lutea*), palo santo (*Bursera graveolens*), velvet shrub (*Waltheria ovata*), Galápagos lantana (*Lantana peduncularis*), croton (*Croton scouleri*), needle-leaf daisy (*Macrea laricifolia*), daisy tree (*Scalesia affinis*), Galápagos cotton (*Gossypium barbadense var. darwinii*), Darwin's daisy (*Darwiniothamnus tenuifolius*), bitterbush (*Castela galapageia*) and Galápagos tomato (*Solanum cheesmaniae*). The trail is also a good place to spot some of Isabela's 11 species of Darwin's finches, including the woodpecker finch, and also flycatchers, cuckoos, anis and mockingbirds. This has had obvious benefits for the feral cats also found here. Orb-web spiders also take advantage of the bushes.

The trail ends at a cinder cone with a panoramic view of Volcán Darwin (it seems everything is named after him here). The dark brown lavas stretching below are some of the roughest in the islands. The coastline can be followed by eye all the way to the Equator, broken only by small patches of green where mangroves thrive.

Tagus is a favourite place to take a *panga* ride along the coast. Wear a hat and suncream. The sandy-coloured cliffs are colonised by marine iguanas, penguins, crabs, sea lions, and, in the crevices outside the bay, colonies of brown noddy terns. It is also an interesting place to snorkel or scuba dive.

Just north of the cove is Punta Tortuga, another small visitor site which has no trail. The long, black, sandy beach is used for nesting by turtles. It has a somewhat melancholy aspect, but makes for interesting beachcombing; finds range from colourful shells to dolphin skeletons and whale vertebrae. The mangroves behind are perhaps the best spot for trying to find the rare mangrove finch. Recent illegal camping by sea cucumber fishermen has threatened the ecology of this quiet refuge.

Black Turtle Beach

A few miles north of Tagus Cove on western Isabela is the lesser know site of Black Turtle Beach. The whole area was uplifted by tectonic activity in 1975, causing many of the mangroves to desiccate. The beach is made of black sand derived from volcanic basalt, and whilst hot for humans it is favoured by nesting turtles and resting sea lions. Large marine iguanas can be found near the shore and at low tide invertebrates and shore birds can be seen. Behind the beach you can find living black, red and white mangroves, and this is one of the few places where the mangrove finch (*Camarhynchus heliobates*) is present, probably the most endangered bird species in the islands.

Puerto Villamil

The only town on Isabela was until recently an isolated human settlement, frequented by fishermen and farmers from the hills. Today, though, tour boats call in and there is a small airstrip. Visitors can see Galápagos tortoises in captivity at the breeding centre, while flamingos may be seen at the lagoon nearby.

From Villamil there are several options for excursions. Take an expedition, partially on horseback, to the active volcano of Sierra Negra, whose 10km crater is second only in size to Ngorongoro; here are steaming fumaroles, vermilion flycatchers and wild donkeys. To the north of Sierra Negra is the recently erupted parasitic cone of Volcán Chico, where you may see Galápagos tortoises in the wild. Closer to town is the Muro de las Lágrimas (the wall of tears), a wall of lava rocks built by convicts when the island was used as a penitentiary.

Tintoreras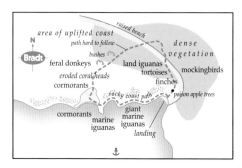

This small islet lies south of Villamil and can be reached by dinghy or on foot at low tide. It is composed of rough, dark lava with fringes of dense mangroves. Near the landing you can see pelicans, the odd penguin and boobies diving off-shore. On one side is a bay with tranquil turquoise waters frequented by sea lions, turtles, marine iguanas and rays. A narrow creek connects to the bay, which is cut off at low tide. This creek is a great place to get close to white-tip reef sharks (*tintoreras* in Spanish), though it is not permitted to swim with them. You should follow the trail carefully as there are many nesting places of marine iguanas who find safety from introduced pests on the main island. On the beaches look for Galápagos clubleaf (*Nolana galapagensis*) plants, a rare endemic in the area.

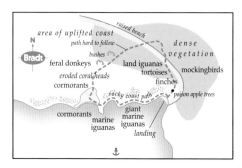

Urvina Bay

The landing on a steep beach can be so wet that you get sodden to your waist. Keep cameras in plastic bags! There are two possibilities for walks: head inland to look for tortoises or along the coast for cormorants. Both trails end up at a raised beach. It is possible to walk the whole circuit in about two hours but, due to the heat and dense vegetation, most visitors do part of each walk.

Go ashore as early as possible. During the rainy season Alcedo tortoises can be found right behind the beach. Also shading themselves below the trees can be seen some of the largest land iguanas in the islands. Large hermit crabs scuttle far inland. Beware of the *manzanillo* or poison apple trees – the whole plant is poisonous and the sap can cause a nasty rash. Tortoises seem to be immune to the poison and thrive on the fruit. Flocks of finches, warblers and mockingbirds inhabit the bushes of *Waltheria*, *Lantana*, Darwin's daisy, white and yellow cordia and palo santo.

The whole area was raised by a volcanic uplift in 1954. That's why you can find rounded pebbles 200m from the shore, plus complete coral heads, sea urchin skeletons, shells, and other marine remains. Today the only sign of life in this bleached white wilderness are feral donkeys.

Going along the coastal path, you negotiate some rough patches of lava inhabited by very large marine iguanas. Eventually you arrive at some uplifted brain corals and a few mangrove trees. Here the flightless cormorant nests. The trail bends around them and heads over the parched uplifted sea floor.

FERNANDINA (NARBOROUGH ISLAND)

As you go west the archipelago gets younger and the volcanoes become more active. Fernandina is the westernmost and the most volcanically active island (indeed, it is one of the most active in the world). Much of it is composed of new lavas with no vegetation; the huge domed cone almost reaches 1,500m.

It is probably the world's largest pristine island, that is, one with no introduced organisms. All the plants and creatures here arrived naturally or evolved in situ. For this reason there is only one landing, and care should be taken not to bring seeds or insects from other islands. The caldera is also impressive, with a depth of 900m and a diameter of about 6km. Visitors are not allowed to climb Fernandina, which is probably a good thing, because of the dangerous aa lava formations (see *Glossary*, page 150) that can cut you to ribbons.

Punta Espinosa

Few boats come here during a week's cruise, so you are fortunate if yours does. This site has an almost indescribable beauty. Punta Espinosa is a promontory of lava and sand. It has a magnificent position, surrounded by the six volcanoes on Isabela that lie across the rich waters of the Bolívar Channel. Feeding frenzies of boobies, dolphins and even whales can be observed in these waters. Fernandina itself has unique attractions: the backdrop of its majestic cone, barren lavas like the surface of Mars, the joy of finding a turtle in a tidepool, the thousands of iguanas, flightless cormorants and penguins... the list goes on and on.

Marine iguanas (*Amblyrhynchus cristatus*) laze on the lava promontory of Punta Espinosa, Fernandina. (DH)

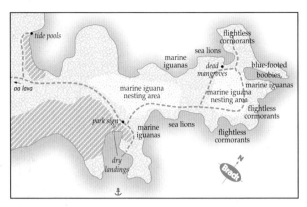

Punta Espinosa means 'Spiny Point' in Spanish. The landing is dry, with a Galápagos National Park Service (GNPS) purpose-built dock, but due to a recent uplift it cannot be reached at low tide, when the rocks make do. At high tide you have to wade through a pool behind the mangroves. Near the park monument is a colony of marine iguanas. Until you look carefully you may not realise how many of these dark reptiles are here. There are literally piles of them! From January to June they breed and lay eggs in the sand. Your guide should make sure no-one strays on to the sands where eggs may be buried. The trail goes out past little beaches with sea lions, and around the point. At the northern tip are nests of the endemic flightless cormorants. These birds stand around drying their vestigial wings and offering nesting material to each other. They are very low in numbers but seem to be unaffected by human visitors. At low tide you can go right out on to the rocks past more marine iguanas and blue-footed boobies.

After visiting the point you can amble among the tide pools to the west. Just behind you can see red, black and white mangroves. The rocks are a favourite place for sally lightfoot crabs, great blue herons and oystercatchers, and in the pools young marine turtles often seek refuge. Galápagos hawks prey on baby iguanas. Land iguanas live at the vegetated summit of Fernandina, but one or two have been found at Punta Espinosa. They seem to have disappeared recently. The elusive mangrove finch has been recorded here, and more commonly yellow warblers.

Another one-way trail goes about 500m inland over blocky and pahoehoe lava, with only the rare sight of a lava lizard or *Brachycereus* cactus. It reaches an impenetrable flow of aa lava, which is like solidified black meringue.

A green turtle (*Chelonia mydas*) in shallow water off Fernandina. (PO)

CONSERVATION

Sea lion (*Zalophus wollebaeki*) (JRG)

In the space of over four centuries since man discovered the 'Enchanted
Islands', he has both exploited the wildlife and damaged the ecology
irreparably. Early visitors such as pirates killed tortoises and left behind
rats, which crept ashore when they careened their ships (hauled them out
for cleaning). Later the whalers took a greater number of tortoises for food
and oil, reducing several subspecies to virtual extinction. Hunters had nearly
exterminated the fur seals by the 1930s. The islands were regarded as a
wilderness and a 'free-for-all' was assumed. Not even the great whales were
safe in the surrounding waters.

Settlers cleared the vegetation for cultivation and pasture, and brought
goats, donkeys and cattle that rapidly stripped the plants on which the reptiles
depended. Putting goats ashore to breed unimpeded was probably even more
destructive than the hunting had been. Introduced cats, dogs and pigs turned
feral and caused havoc with the native fauna, especially ground-nesting birds such
as the dark-rumped petrel. These imported mammals still could threaten the
penguins and cormorants today.

Island ecosystems are extremely vulnerable to organisms introduced from
elsewhere. The native creatures are specialised to the simplified habitats and
unused to predators, so they cannot compete with aggressive intruders. During
the early 20th century even scientists contributed to the decimation, with their
passion for 'collecting'; they removed some of the last remaining tortoises
from islands where they later became extinct. Fortunately the adverse effect
of humans has now been recognised and attempts are being made to reverse
this situation.

THE GALÁPAGOS NATIONAL PARK

In 1934, the Ecuadorian government passed the first laws protecting fauna
in the archipelago, making it necessary to obtain permits to land, and collect
specimens. The idea to set aside certain islands as a reserve was put forward
in 1936, but nothing practical was done until two decades later. Ecuador
was a 'developing' country with limited resources, and during World War II
it had other priorities. In 1957, a UNESCO fact-finding mission was invited
by Ecuador to assess the status of the wildlife and advise on the creation of
reserves.

In 1959, 100 years after the publication of Darwin's *On the Origin of Species*,
a special body, the Charles Darwin Foundation (CDF) for the Galápagos
Islands, was created. The CDF headquarters was based in Brussels. It was
an international foundation, but recognised by the Ecuadorian government.
The authorities understood that the archipelago had limited potential for
agriculture, that the islands possessed a unique flora and fauna of outstanding
importance, and that there was a great potential for tourism. That same year,
the Ecuadorian government declared all areas of the archipelago to be a national
park, except those parts already colonised. In those days the prevailing attitude
was to exploit nature. It was a hard task to convince colonists and Ecuador's

Galápagos National Park Rules

- Due to their unique nature, the plants, animals and rocks must remain undisturbed so as not to cause changes of any kind. It is not permitted to take anything from the islands, with the exception of photos.
- Each island of the archipelago has flora, fauna and natural features unique to that island, so that any introduction of foreign organisms, such as animals, seeds, plants and insects, can cause serious problems. Your collaboration to prevent this happening is paramount.
- The animals in Galápagos *must not be handled* or touched for your personal security and because this will rapidly change their behaviour and destroy their fearlessness towards people.
- The endemic and native fauna of Galápagos have their own natural way of feeding, for which reason no food of any kind must be given to them, as this can be very harmful.
- Each year thousands of visitors come to Galápagos. Can you imagine what would happen if each one took a shell, or a plant, or disturbed an animal . . ?
- Marine birds, when disturbed or frightened, quickly abandon their nests, allowing eggs and chicks to fall to the ground, or leaving them exposed to the sun; for this reason a distance of at least 2m should be kept when observing such birds.
- When visiting the islands, it is prohibited to bring in pets or other animals, as such endanger native flora and fauna of Galápagos.
- To maintain the natural state of the islands, no living organism may be brought in from the mainland or transported between islands. Plants, seeds, insects, plagues and diseases are highly dangerous to this fragile ecosystem.
- The visitor sites and trails of the Galápagos National Park are clearly marked to guarantee your safety. *You must stay on the trails.*
- Fishing is not allowed aboard tourist boats.
- Rubbish of any kind can interfere with nature's processes and destroys the natural beauty of the islands. Do not dispose of waste around visitor sites, nor in the sea, nor close to the coasts. Sea lions may pick up tin cans whilst playing and cut their snouts; plastics may be eaten by sea turtles, who then die with their digestive tracts blocked. You must leave nothing on the islands, with the exception of your footprints.
- On the inhabited islands you will be able to buy handicrafts of Galápagos made from wood, pottery, etc. Buying souvenirs made of black coral, turtleshell, sea lion teeth and shells goes against the principles of conservation.
- Graffiti of any kind on rocks, cliffs, etc, is a sign of ignorance and lack of respect and destroys the scenery. Remember, 'Your immortality is not more important than the natural beauty of the islands'.
- It is not allowed to light fires or to smoke within the bounds of the park. Remember that a fire can be started by a discarded match or cigarette butt.
- If you wish to camp in the designated camping sites, you must obtain the permission from the park authorities.
- Professional filming must be with special authorisation given by the Ecuadorian Institute of Forestry and Protected Areas (INEFAN).

Ministry of Agriculture and Fisheries (which managed national parks at that time) that it was worthwhile to conserve the islands so that foreign tourists would come and help pay for the preservation. Fortunately, a few influential individuals became convinced that this was the way forward.

In the early 1960s, the first objective of the foundation was to build a research station on one of the islands. In 1964, this was completed at Academy Bay on Santa Cruz. Inevitably it was called the Charles Darwin Research Station (CDRS). In the early days, the scientists spent much of their time trying to eradicate introduced species. The other roles of the staff were scientific research and education.

Scientists from the Charles Darwin Research Station ring and record a Galápagos hawk (*Buteo galapagoensis*) on Española. (PO)

In 1968 the Galápagos National Park Service (GNPS) was set up, to administer the day-to-day running of the park, and take over much of the conservation and eradication programmes. The two organisations have worked in tandem ever since. In 1974, the first 'master plan' laid down the strategy of creating zones of different usage, together with the rules and regulations to enforce and protect the zones. Some zones would only be open to scientists – pristine islands with no introduced organisms such as Fernandina (except for one small site). The rules for visitors and tourist boats were implemented. Between 1973 and 1978, the number of tourists rose from 8,000 to 10,000 annually. The steady increase each year reflected the growing global interest in ecotourism. In 1979, UNESCO declared the Galápagos Islands a World Heritage Site. This meant that international aid in the form of funds and expertise would be made available to help protect the islands.

REPAIRING THE DAMAGE

The park service had an early success with the eradication of goats from small islands like Santa Fé, Plazas, Española, Rábida and Pinta but in those days resources and money were limited. Though tourists paid an entrance fee, little money made its way back to the GNPS from Quito, the capital of Ecuador. The CDRS also relied on donations from organisations such as the Worldwide Fund for Nature (WWF), the Smithsonian and the Frankfurt Zoological Society.

The next task was to captive-breed the endangered tortoises and land iguanas. A breeding programme began at the CDRS. By 2010, 1,400 young tortoises were repatriated to Española and are now reproducing there, and land iguanas were returned to parts of Santa Cruz where dogs had wiped them out. On the island of Pinta, sadly there remained only one male tortoise, 'Lonesome George'. Much publicity has been given to attempts to encourage George to breed in captivity, but as yet these have been unsuccessful. Although his female companions from nearby Isabela Island have laid eggs, they were not fertile. In 2010, 29 sterile hybrid adult giant tortoises were put on Pinta to act as herbivorous habitat cleaners, and the next step will involve re-populating the island with a reproductive tortoise population. By 2010, over 4,000 young tortoises had been returned to their roots in the wild and many of them are now reproducing and adding to their populations.

From 1998 to 2006 Project Isabela operated on the islands of Pinta, Santiago and northern Isabela. This project was aimed at restoring the islands' ecosystems by removing feral goats, donkeys and pigs. The final stage was northern Isabela, where over 100,000 goats had had a devastating effect, but hopefully the vegetation will grow back now that they have been removed. The park's latest ecosystem project is Project Floreana; this will be the first time that an inhabited island has been restored.

TOURISM AND EDUCATION

The other brief of the park service and CDRS was to educate both locals and visitors about the fragile ecology of the archipelago. Tourist numbers increased annually from 45,000 in the late 1980s to an estimated 180,000 in 2009. The airstrip was extended on Baltra so jets could arrive daily and a new airport was constructed on San Cristóbal. The CDRS became an important site for tourists to visit and see the tortoises in the breeding corrals. The approach was to make the Galápagos a 'living laboratory', not a zoo.

Blue-footed booby chick (*Sula nebouxi*) (PO)

Since then the park has opened interpretation centres on both San Cristóbal and Isabela. The naturalist guides, of whom there are three categories, are all trained by the GNPS with help from CDRS personnel. They not only inform and entertain tour boat passengers but also act as unofficial park wardens, keeping an eye on tourists to make sure the park rules are obeyed. Tourists have to keep close to their guide and walk only on specially designated trails. They must not interfere with the wildlife. Despite the increasing visitor numbers it is a system that works, and most studies assessing the impact on the fauna by tourists conclude that the islands and animals are not seriously affected. There is inevitably some erosion to geological features, so in heavily visited places like Bartolomé, the park wardens have built wooden steps.

In the early days of tourism, the guides were often enthusiastic foreign science graduates. Over the last two decades a greater proportion of Ecuadorians have become professional licensed guides, including some who were born in the Galápagos. Fortunately conservation features in the Galápagos school curriculum, for that is where the future lies.

MARINE CONSERVATION

There is no point in protecting the land habitats of Galápagos if the marine environment is pillaged. Seas are the lifeblood of the archipelago; the park would cease to exist without the rich surrounding waters, with their plankton, fish, seabirds and mammals. The total coastline of the islands is greater than mainland Ecuador.

Pacific green turtle (*Chelonia mydas agassisi*) (JRG)

The scientific community had always hoped that legislation would be passed to protect the marine environment. Surprisingly, it was not until 1986 that a presidential decree was issued establishing a Galápagos Marine Resources Reserve. UNESCO then declared this area a World Heritage Site in 2001. This included the entire water surrounding the islands to a distance of 15 nautical miles (about 70,000km^2). This was quite a victory for conservation, as the original recommendation in the master plan was for only 3 nautical miles (5km^2). It certainly looked good on paper, but management of such an area proved difficult for the GNPS on a limited budget. Their patrol boats were frequently out of action, and when a fast new patrol boat was donated, they could not always afford the fuel to make use of it.

The late 1980s saw a boom in tourism and the number of yachts operating. This attracted migrants from poorer parts of Ecuador, not all of them enlightened by the conservation ethic that most *Galapagueños* had, resulting in a localised population explosion. Population numbers continue to rise, from about 4,000 in 1978 to an estimated 30,000 at the time of writing.

FROM SEA CUCUMBERS TO SHARK FINS

In the early 1990s outside entrepreneurs found a market in the Orient for sea cucumbers (a relative of sea urchins). These ugly invertebrates are thought to be aphrodisiacs and can fetch high prices in Asia. Industrial fishing companies from mainland Ecuador were used to recruit labour to collect the *pepinos del mar* as they are called in Spanish.

Sea cucumbers need to be boiled and processed within hours of collection, so illegal camps were set up clandestinely on the beaches of Isabela and the pristine jewel of Galápagos, Fernandina. Eventually word got out and the authorities clamped down, with the help of the navy. *Pepino* collection was outlawed. However, due to the enormous sums of money involved, the fishermen used the press and campaigned for their rights to collect *pepinos*. Having over-fished lobsters in previous decades, they wanted an alternative livelihood. The situation degenerated into a war between *pepino* fishermen and the tourism lobby who were portrayed as misguided 'greens'.

The authorities relented and issued fishing quotas to the *pepino*-collectors but these were soon exceeded by the million and the disputes continued. In December 1994, the CDRS and National Park offices were besieged by demonstrators, and the station director was subjected to threats. Tortoises were killed on Isabela, and the world's press became interested in the story. UNESCO threatened to put the archipelago on its list of sites in peril, which would have embarrassed the government.

Fishing on a local 'artisan' basis has always been a part of the human side of the islands. It was done by locals on small, primitive craft and could be called sustainable. At the same time as the sea cucumber dispute, the rapacious international fishing industry was moving closer to the islands' supposedly protected waters. Japanese, Taiwanese and Costa Rican long-line fishing

---

Conservation organisations and other information

Charles Darwin Foundation
www.darwinfoundation.org

Darwin Online
www.darwin-online.org.uk

Ecuador Travel
www.ecuador.travel

Galápagos Conservancy (US Friends of Galápagos)
www.galapagos.org

Galápagos Conservation Trust (UK Friends of Galápagos)
www.savegalapagos.org

Galápagos National Park
www.galapagospark.org

---

boats and tuna boats were coming as close as they dared. Even when caught, they paid a fine and then carried on. Once they had over-fished lobsters and sea cucumbers they moved on to shark fins and even sea lion genitalia for the Oriental market.

THE FUTURE

In 1997 a dramatic change occurred. Concerned local residents from all walks of life, together with mainland organisations, petitioned their local senators and the president. Conflict became consensus over the issue of the marine reserve. Subsequent changes in government and presidents (there were three in one day in February 1997), eventually stabilised, and in 1998, a new special law for the Galápagos was passed by presidential decree and ratified by Congress. The law addressed three big issues: immigration restriction, quarantine of introduced organisms, and fisheries. Two main points of legislation resulted.

Firstly, the marine reserve became a legally protected area, managed by the Galápagos National Park Service (together with local institutions). Secondly, the marine reserve area was extended (from 15 to 40 nautical miles), around the whole archipelago, with only tourism and local artisanal fishing permitted within this area. This outlawed industrial fishing of all types. Now the Galápagos are second only to the Great Barrier Reef National Park of Australia in terms of the size of marine area protected (130,000km^2).

The fame of the Galápagos impacts on the islands in many different ways. In 1999, when a volcanic eruption began on southern Isabela, the park authorities decided to evacuate some of the rare giant tortoises. This prompted a media frenzy which was repeated in 2001 when a supply tanker, the *Jessica*, hit the rocks of San Cristóbal and caused an oil spill. The extent of the damage is still being assessed but it could have been a lot worse. Lessons in emergency response were certainly learnt.

Nearly a decade later in 2007 President Rafael Correa declared the Galápagos 'at risk', and UNESCO put the archipelago on the List of World Heritage Sites in Danger, as a response to reports by scientists about the rapid growth of local population, tourism and habitat damage. In 2010 UNESCO controversially removed the islands from the 'In Danger' list, but much work needs to be done.

Revenues from visitor park fees ($100 per person) are now re-allocated between the GNPS and the local councils (to use to improve the environment and tourist facilities), with smaller portions going to the quarantine of introduced species, to Ecuador's national reserves and to the navy.

The quarantine aspect is crucial, for the biggest threat to the native organisms is introduced pests and plants. Since the 1990s, we have seen vicious wasps spread throughout the whole archipelago, a mystery illness attack the tortoises on Santa Cruz (possibly a virus or parasitic worms) and a parasite strike the Darwin's finches, surely one of the islands' most famous inhabitants.

Today one of the main concerns is still control of invasive pests, but there have been recent successes such as the biological control of cottony cushion scale, a parasite on native plants. The other tasks are to find alternative livelihoods for the local fishermen or sustainable fishing methods that can be used in the reserve, and to improve waste management, migration control and sustainable tourism. The greatest challenge ahead is to find a balance whereby the presence of humans does not affect the biodiversity, but rather contributes to its preservation.

El Barranco (Prince Philip's Steps) on Genovesa Island: small-scale, carefully managed tourism using environmentally friendly boats remains the best way to keep the islands' economy sound, and hence fund conservation for the future. (DH)

GLOSSARY

Aa lava Hawaiian/geological term for angular, rough-textured basaltic lava. It results from being 'bulldozed' rather than flowing gently. Impossible to walk over.

Avifauna The part of the fauna composed of birds only.

Baleen whalebone The transverse plates made of keratin which hang from the upper jaws of toothless whales. The arrangement of the baleen plates with their hairy edges forms the filter-feeding sieve of the baleen whales.

Basalt A dense, dark volcanic rock commonly found at oceanic volcanoes. Composed of material originating in the earth's mantle.

Convection current A moving current caused by the transmission of heat from one part of a liquid or gas to another.

Dimorphism Showing variants.

Endemic An organism that occurs naturally within the specified area and nowhere else in the world.

Epiphyte Plant growing on another, rather than being rooted in the soil.

Garúa A fine mist which condenses at approximately 300–600m and is a typical feature of the Galápagos Islands between the months of July and December.

Lanugo The natal fur of members of the pinniped family (seals). Also seen in some other mammals (including foetal humans), it is shed early in life.

Morph A variant.

Nictitating membrane A transparent membrane forming a third eyelid which can be drawn over the eye to protect it. Common in reptiles, birds, some sharks and amphibians.

Pahoehoe Ropey or smooth-textured basaltic lava. The lava flows gently and the surface cools first so the friction of the layers produces various shapes like ropes, intestines or ripples.

Pelagic Organisms that inhabit the open ocean, such as albatross or whales.

Pinna A fold of skin forming the external part of the ear.

Pinniped Group of marine mammals with flipper-like front and rear limbs. The group includes the sea lions, fur seals, true seals and walruses.

Precocial young Young animals or birds which are born in a partially independent state.

Semi-palmated Partly webbed.

Stereoscopic vision Two views at slightly different angles from each eye, producing a combined 3D image with perception of depth.

Thigmotactic Seeking body contact.

Classification

To avoid confusion through the use of common names when identifying living things, scientists around the world refer to animals or plants by scientific names. This binomial (two-part) naming system, given in Latin, was first used by an eminent Swedish botanist, Carl Linnaeus, in the 1750s. In order to firmly establish an organism's position within the living world it is classified according to a hierarchy of names, becoming more and more specific until the animal or plant in question has been isolated from all other living things. For example, the Galápagos fur seal and the Galápagos flightless cormorant are classified in the following ways:

Galápagos fur seal		**Galápagos flightless cormorant**	
Kingdom	Animalia	Kingdom	Animalia
Phylum	Chordata	Phylum	Chordata
Class	Mammalia	Class	Aves
Order	Carnivora	Order	Pelecaniformes
Family	Otariidae	Family	Phalacrocoracidae
Subfamily	Arctocephalinae	Genus	*Phalacrocorax*
Genus	*Arctocephalus*	Species	*harrisi*
Species	*galapagoensis*		

In the text the whole classification has not been used; only the last two names – the genus and species. These are written in italics to denote their Latin origin and, as standard, the genus name always begins in upper case and the specific name (species) always in lower case.

The derivation of the scientific name is not always straightforward but in the case of the Galápagos fur seal, for example, *Arctocephalus* translates as 'bear head' and is a reference to the similarities between the skulls of fur seals and bears, while the *galapagoensis* tells us that the animal is from the Galápagos. Sometimes organisms are named after people, as in the case of the flightless cormorant which was named after ornithologist Michael Harris. Nevertheless, the species name still appears in lower case. The humpback whale's scientific name is *Megaptera novaeangliae*, which derives from the Greek megas meaning large and *pteron* meaning wing or fin, then the Latin *novus* for new and the old English *angliae* for England. We could translate this as the large-finned New Englander, named after its huge pectoral fins and the fact that it was known mostly from the New England coast of North America when it was named.

Sometimes a trinomial is used, consisting of three names. This refers to a subspecies or race of a species. For example, the scientific name of 'Lonesome George', the last living member of the subspecies of giant tortoise from the island of Pinta, is *Geochelone elephantopus abingdoni*. All Galápagos giant tortoises are in the same species, *Geochelone elephantopus*, but they are now divided into 11 subspecies (which one day may further evolve to be sufficiently different from each other that they can be considered 11 full species). The subspecies name *abingdoni* refers to the island of Pinta, whose English name is Abingdon. If an organism's name is only known as far as genus level, using land iguana as an example, then its scientific name will be written *Conolophus sp.* If the text refers to more than one species of land iguana, it will be written *Conolophus spp.*

FURTHER READING

Angermeyer, J *My Father's Island* Nelson. 1998

Beebe, W *Galápagos – World's End* C P Putman, London, New York. 1924

Castro, I and Phillips, A *A Guide to the Birds of the Galápagos* Christopher Helm/A C Black. 1996

Cribb, J *Subtidal Galápagos, Exploring the Waters of Darwin's Islands.* Camden House Publishing Ltd. 1986

Darwin, C *On the Origin of Species* John Murray, London. 1859

Darwin, C *The Voyage of the Beagle. Journal of researches into the Natural History and Geology of the Countries visited during the Voyage round the World of H.M.S. 'Beagle' under command of Captain FitzRoy, R.N.* John Murray, London. 1845

De Roy, T *Galápagos, Preserving Darwin's Legacy* A & C Black, London. 2009

Estes, G and Grant, T *Darwin in Galápagos, Footsteps to a New World* Princeton University Press. 2009

Fitter, J & D and Hosking, D *Wildlife of Galápagos* Collins. 2007

Grant, P R *Ecology and Evolution of Darwin's Finches* Princeton University Press, New Jersey. 1986

Grove, J S, Garcia, S and Massey, S *Lista de los peces de Galápagos* Boletin Científico y Técnico, Instituto Nacional de Pesca, Guayaquil, Ecuador. 1984

Grove, J S and Lavenberg, R J *The Fishes of the Galápagos Islands* Stanford University Press, Stanford, California. 1997

Harris, M P *A Field Guide to the Birds of the Galápagos* Collins, London. 1974

Harrison P *Seabirds an Identification Guide* Christopher Helm, London. 1993

Hickin, N *Animal Life of the Galápagos, an illustrated guide* Ferrendune Books. 1979

Hickman, J *The Enchanted Islands: The Galápagos Discovered* Anthony Nelson Ltd. 1985

Humann, P *Reef Fish Identification Galápagos* Libri Mundi, Ecuador. 1993

Jackson, M H *Galápagos, A Natural History Guide* The University of Calgary Press, Calgary. 1993

Lack, D *Darwin's Finches* Cambridge University Press, London. 1947

McMullen, C K *Flowering Plants of the Galápagos* Cornell University Press. 1999

Merlen, G *A Field Guide to the Fishes of the Galápagos* Wilmot Books, London. 1988

Moore, A, and Moore, T *Guide to the visitor sites of Parque Nacional Galápagos* Servicio Parque Nacional, Galápagos, Ecuador. 1987

Moore, T *Galápagos Islands Lost in Time* Viking Press, New York. 1980

Moorhead, A *Darwin and the Beagle* Penguin, Harmondsworth, England. 1971

Nelson, B *Galápagos: Islands of Birds* Longmans Green and Co Ltd. 1968

Nelson, J B *The Sulidae* Oxford University Press, London. 1978

Oxford, P and Watkins, G *Galápagos, Both Sides of the Coin* Imagine Books, New York. 2009

Perry, R *Galápagos* (Key Environments). Pergamon Press Ltd, Oxford. 1984

Ryan, P R *Oceanus*, the International Magazine of Marine Science and Policy. Vol 30, No 2. Woods Hole Oceanographic Institute. 1987

Schofield, E K *Field Guide to Some Common Galápagos Plants* Ohio State University Research Foundation, Columbus. 1970

Schofield, E K *Plants of the Galápagos Islands* Universe Books. 1984

Schönitzer, K *Galápagos Plants* Contribution Number 172 of the Charles Darwin Foundation

Steadman, D W and Zousmer, S *Galápagos discovery on Darwin's Islands* Smithsonian Institution Press. 1988

Thornton, I *Darwin's Islands: A Natural History of the Galápagos Islands* Natural History Press, Garden City, New York. 1971

Treherne, J E *The Galápagos Affair* Jonathan Cape, London. 1983

Weiner, J *The Beak of the Finch: A Story of Evolution in Our Time* Vintage. 1995

Wellington, G M *The Galápagos Coastal Marine Environments* Charles Darwin Research Station, Galápagos. 1975

Wiggins, I L and Porter, D M *Flora of the Galápagos Islands* Stanford University Press, Stanford, California. 1971

Wittmer, M *Floreana* Anthony Nelson Ltd. 1989

INDEX

Page numbers in *italics* refer to illustrations

Abudefduf troschelii 101
acacias 13, 22
Acanthuridae 102
Aetobatus narinari 107, 108
Agraulis vanilla galapagoensis 27, 29
albatross, waved *49*, 70–1
Alsophis sp 49
Amblyrhuncus cristatus 45, 95
American oystercatcher 80
Anas bahamensis galapagoensis 79
angelfish 98, 99
ani, amooth-billed 54
Anisotremus interruptus 98, 99
Anous stolidus 74, *75*
Arctocephalus galapagoensis 85, 89
Ardea Herodias 51
Ardea Herodias 76, *77*
Argiope argentata 32
arid zone 11–13
Arothron meleagris 102
arthropods 28
Asilo de la Paz 126–7
Asio flammeus galapagoensis 57
Atriplex peruviana 11
Atriplex peruviana 18
Aulostomidae 101
Avicennia germinans 8, 20

Bachas Beach 110
Bainbridge Rocks 80
Balaenoptera acutorostrata 91
Balaenoptera borealis 91
Balaenoptera edeni 91
Balaenoptera physalus 91
Balistidae 103
Baltra 43
Barrington Island 117–18
Bartolomé 7, 13, 58, 104, 129–31
batfish, red-lipped 100
Batis maritima 11
bats 92
beach morning glory 16, *25*
birds 49–82
　land 51–7
　sea 58–75
　shore 76–82
bitterbush 13, 22
Black Turtle Beach 137
Black Turtle Cove 111, *112*
black-necked stilt *79*
blenny, four-eyed 100
Bodianus diplotaenia 96, 97
boobies 59–64
　blue-footed 13, 60–1
　Nazca (masked) 63–4
　red-footed 62–3
Brachycereus nesioticus 11, *15*
Brachygastra lecheguana 29
Bubulcus ibis 78

Buccaneer Cove 127–8
Bursera graveolens 13, *23*, 24
Buteo galapagoensis 56, 57
Butorides sundevalli 78
butterflies 27, 29–31, 101

cacti 26
　candelabra 11, 26
　lava 11, *15*, 26
　Opuntia 10, 26, 39, 56
　prickly pear 11, 26
Caleta Tortuga Negra 111
Camarhynchus parvulus 53
Carcharhinus galapagensis 104
Carcharhinus limbatus 104
Carnegie Ridge 3
carpenter bee *28, 29*
Casmerodias albus 78
Castela galapageia 13
Castela galapageia 13, 22
cat's claw 13
centipedes *28*, 32
Centruoides exsul 32
Cerro Brujo 121
Cerro Colorado Visitor Centre 121
Cerro Crocker 113
Cerro de las Tijeretas 120
Cerro Dragón 113
Cerro Pajas 71
Certhidea olivacea 53
Chaetodontidae 101
Chamaesyce amplexicaulis 22
Charadriiformes 58
Charles Darwin Foundation for the Galápagos Islands 6
Charles Darwin Research Station 6, 111
Chelonia mydas agassisi 40, 41–2
Chiococca alba 13
Chiton goodalli 93
cinchona 14
climate 3–4
clubleaf 11, 18
Coccyzus melacopyphus 54
Coenobita compressa 93
Colnett, James 5
Conocarpus erecta 8, 20
Conolophus pallidus 43
Conolophus subcristatus 43, *44*
conservation 141–9
　marine 146
　organisations 148
Conway Bay 113
coral, uplifted *9*
cormorant, flightless, Galápagos 67
cotton, Galápagos *17*, 23
Cowley, Ambrose 5
crabs 11, 93
　Sally lightfoot 93
crake, paint-billed 56

Croton scouleri 13
Cryptocarpus pyriformis 11, 20
Ciotophaga sulcirostris 54
cuckoo, dark-billed 54
cutleaf daisy 23
Cyathea weatherbyana 14

daisy tree 23
Dampier, William 5
damselfish *100*, 101
Danaus plexippus 30
Daphne Major 115
Darwin Bay 131–2
Darwin Island 8
Darwin, Charles 2, 6
Darwin's daisy 23, *25*
Darwiniothamnus tenuifolius 23, *25*
Dasyatididae 108
Dasyatis brevis 108
Davis, Edward 5
Delphinus delphis 90
Dendroica petechia 54
Dialommus fuscus 100
dolphins 90–1
dove, Galápagos *50*, 56
Dragon Hill 113

Echeneis spp 102
egrets 78
Egretta thula 78
El Junco Lagoon 120
El Niño 4, 13, 95
Elizabeth Bay 135
Encope micrpora 95
epiphytes 13, *25*
Española 1, 8, 46, 47, 70, 86, 122–4
Espumilla Beach 128
Eucidaris thouarsii 95
evolution 2

Fernandina 1, 3, 43, 45, 58, 67, 91, 92, 138–40
finches 13, 52, *53*
FitzRoy, Robert 6
flamingo, Caribbean 11, 80–2
Floreana 5, 13, 47, 58, 80, 124–7
flycatchers 54, 55
Fregata magnificens 64
Fregata minor 64
Frigatebird Hill 120
frigatebirds 64–7
　great 64–7
　magnificent 64–7

Galápagos National Park 6, 142–4
　rules 143
Gallinula chloropus 56
Gardner Bay 86, 123–4
garúa 13, 86
Gasteracantha cancriformis 32

gecko 48
Genovesa 8, 57, 64, 68, 72, 131–2
Geochelone elephantopus 33, 34, 35–9
Geochelone elephantopus abingdoni
  35
Geochelone elephantopus hoodensis 37
Geochelone elephantopus porteri 14
Geochelone elephantopus
  vandenburghi 34
geology 1–3
Geospiza fortis 53
Geospiza magnirostris 53
Geospiza scandens 53
Globicephala macrorhyncus 90
Gossypium darwinii 17, 23
Grapsus grapsus 93
grey matplant 13, 21
grunt, yellow-tailed *98*
guava, Galápagos 13–14
guava, introduced 14
gulls 72–3

Hadruoides maculatus galapagoensis
  32
Hadruroides maculates galapagoensis
  28
Haematopus palliatus 80
hawk, Galápagos *56*, 57
Heliaster spp 95
heliotrope, seaside 11, *16*, 17
Heliotropium curassavicum 11
herbs 16–17
herons 76–8
  great blue 76, *77*
  lava 78
Heteropoda venatoria 32
Heteroscelus incanus 79–80
highland zone 13–14
  plants 24–5
Himantopus himantopus 79
Hippomane mencinella 23, 24
history 5–6
hogfish, Mexican 96
Holocanthus passer 98
Hood Island 122–4

iguana, land *10*, 13
iguana, marine 11
inkberry 11
insects 29–31
invertebrates 27–32
Ipomoea pes-caprae 11
Ipomoea pescaprae 16, *25*
Isabela 36, 43, 58, 64, 80, 91,
  134–8
Isla Lobos 122
Isla Mosquera 116
Isla Mosquera 86, 116
island landings 109–40

Jasminocereus thouarsii 11

Kicker Rock 122

La Galapaguera 121
La Loberia 126
La Niña 4
Labridae 101
Laguncularia racemosa 8, 20
land iguana 43–5

lantana, Galápagos *18*, 24
Lantana peduncularis 18, 24
Larus fuliginosus 72, *73*
Larus furcatus 72, *73*
Lasiurus borealis brachyotis 92
Lasiurus cinereus 92
Laterallus spilonotus 56
Latrodectus apicalis 32
lava *8*
leatherleaf 11
Leatherleaf *18*
Leguminosae mimosaceae 22
Leocarpus pinnatifidus 23
Léon Dormido 122
Leptotes parrhasioides 29
littoral zone 8
  plants 16–20
lizards 43–8
  lava 13, *45*, 47
'Lonesome George' *35*, 36
Los Gemelos *24*, 114
Lycopodium 14, 24
Lytechinus semituberculatus 95

Malaspina, Alessandro 5
mammals 83–92
mangroves 8, 11, *18*, 19–20
Manta hamiltoni 107
manzanillo *23*, 24
Marchena 47
marine iguana 45–6, 95
martin, Galápagos 55
Maytenus octogona 11
Maytenus octogona 18
mealy leaf 11, 18
Media Luna 113
Megabalanus galapaganus 93
Megaptera novaeangliae 91
Miconia 14
Microlophus spp 45, 47
Microsphathodon dorsalis 100
milkberry 13
milkwort 16
Mirador de la Baronesa 126
mockingbirds 13, 51–4
Mola mola 102
mollugo 11

Lava lizard (*Microlophus sp*) (PO)

Mollugo flavescens 11, 20
moorhen 56
morning glory 11
moss 14
moths 30–31
Myiarchus magnirostris 54, *55*

Neocrex erythrops 56
Neoscona oaxacensis 32
Nesomimus spp 51–4
Nesoryzomys fernandinae 92
Nesoryzomys narboroughii 92
Nesoryzomys swarthy 92
noddy, brown 74, *75*
Nolana galapagensis 11
Nolana galapagoensis 18
North Seymour 43, 64, 116–17
Nyctanassa violacea 76

Oceanites gracilis 71
Oceanodroma castro 71
Oceanodroma tethys 71–2
Ocypode gaudichaudii 93
Odontoceti 90–1
Ogcocephalus darwinii 100
Orcinus orca 90, 91
orthopterans 31
Oryzomys bauri 92
owl, barn 57
owl, short-eared 57

Pacific green turtles *40*, 41–2
painted locust 31
palo santo 13, *23*, 24
parrotfish *99*, 101
Passiflora foetida 21
passion flower 21
pega-pega 13
Pelamis platurus 49
Pelecaniformes 58
Pelecanus occidentalis urinator 74–5
pelican, brown 74–5
penguin, Galápagos 58–9, *96*
Pentacerater cumingi 93
petrel, Galápagos 71
petunia, shore 17
Phaethon aethereus 68–9
Phalacrocorax harrisi 67
phalaropes 79
Philodryas sp 49
Phoebastria irrorata 49, 70–1
Phoebis sennae marcellina 29
Phoenicopterus ruber 80–2
Phyllodactylus spp 48
Physeter macrocephalus 90
Pinnacle Rock 58
Pinta 36, 47
pintail, white-cheeked 79
Pinzón 36, 47
Pisonia floribunda 13
plants 15–26
Platyspiza crassirostris 53
Playa Ochoa 122
Plaza Sur 86
Polistes versicolor 29
Polygala spp 16
Portulaca oleracea 22
Post Office Bay 125–6
Prince Philip's Steps 72, 132

Prionurus latclavius 103
Procellariformes 58
Progne modesta 55
Project Isabela 145
Pseudorca crassidens 90
Psidium galapageium 13
Psidium guayava 14
Pterodroma phaeopygia 71
Puerto Baquerizo Moreno 120
Puerto Chino 121
Puerto Egas 86, 89, 129
Puerto Villamil 137
pufferfish 102
Puffinus subalaris 71
puncture vine 22, 25
Punta Albemarle 134–5
Punta Cormorant 124–5
Punta Espinosa 45, 139–40
Punta Moreno 135–6
Punta Pitt 120–1
Punta Suárez 122–3
purslane 22
purslane, sea 11, *21*
Pyrocephalus rubinus 54, *55*

Rábida 80, 86, 132–3
rail, Galápagos 56
raptors 57
rats 92
Rattus norvegicus 92
Rattus rattus 92
rays 103, 107–8
remora 102
reptiles 33–48
Rhincodon typus 106, 107
Rhinoptera steindachneri 107
Rhizophora mangle 8, *18*, 19–20
saltbush 11, 19
saltwort 11
San Cristóbal 13, 46, 47, 64, 119–20
Santa Cruz 8, *12*, 35, 43, 57, 80, 111
Santa Fé 92, 117–18
Santiago 13, 36, 80, 127–9
Scaevola plumieri 11
Scalesia 12, 13, *23*, *24*
Scaridae 101
Schistocerca melanocera 31
Scolopendra galapagoensis 28
Scolopendra galapagoensis 32
scorpions *28*, 32
Scutea pauciflora 24
sea horse 101
sea lions *83*, *84*, 85–9, *141*
sea purslane 16
sedge 17
Sesuvium 11, *21*
Sesuvium spp 16
sharks 103–7
shearwater, Galápagos 71
shrimps, brine 11
shrubs 18
snails 28
snakes 13, 48
snapper, Jordan's *99*
Solanum cheesmaniae 21, *25*
Sombrero Chino 133–4

South Plaza *10*, 43, 68, 118–19
Sphenisciformes 58
Spheniscus mendiculus 58
Sphyrna lewini 104
Sphyroides annulatus 102
spiders 32
spurge 22
Stenella coeruleoalba 91
Stenella longirostris 91
storm petrels 71–2
Sula granti 63–4
Sula nebouxii excisa 60
Sula sula websteri 62–3
Sullivan Bay 129
sunfish 102
surgeonfish 102
   yellow-tailed 103
Syngathidae 101

Tagus Cove 136–7
tattler, wandering 79–80
Tetraodontidae 102
Thalassoma lucasanum 101
thorn shrub 24
Tintoreras 138
Tiquilia nesiotica 13, 21
tomato, Galápagos 21, *25*
Tortoise Reserve 113–14
tortoises *33*, *34*, 35–9
Triaendon obesus 105, 107
Tribulus cistoides 22, *25*
triggerfish 103
tropicbird, red-billed 68–9
Trox suberosus 29
trumpetfish 101
tortoises *14*
Tursiops truncates 91
Turtle Bay 114
Tyto punctatissima 57

Ulva lobata 95
Urbanus dorantes 29
Urvina Bay 138

Vanessa carye 30
Vanessa virginensis 30
velvet shrub 24
Volcán Alcedo 35–6, 134
volcanoes *9*

Waltheria ovata 24
warbler, yellow 54
warblers 13
   yellow-crowned night 76
Wasmannia auropunctata 29
Watkins, Patrick 5
Whale Bay 113
whales 90–1
whaling 5
Wittmer, Margaret 6
wrasses *98*, 101

Xylocopa darwinii 28, 29

Zalophus wollebaeki 83, *84*, *141*
Zanthoxylum fagara 13
Zenaida galapagoensis 50, 56

SCIENTIFIC NAME	ENGLISH	SPANISH
Plants	Plants	Plantas
Acacia rorudiana	Acacia	Algarrobo, Acacia
Alternanthera spp	Alternanthera	Alternántera
Brachycereus nesioticus	Lava cactus	Cactillo de lava negra
Bursera malacophylla	Palo santo	Palo santo
Capsicum galapagense	Galápagos pepper	Ají de monte
Castela galapageia	Castela/Bitterbush	Castela
Chamaesyce amplexicaulis	Spurge	Chamaesyce
Chamaesyce spp	Chamaesyce	Chamaesyce
Croton scouleri	Croton	Chala, Mosquero
Cyathea weatherbyana	Tree fern	Chontillo, Helecho árbol
Darwiniothamnus tenuifolius	Darwin's daisy	Darwiniotamus
Epidendrum spicatum	Orchid	Orquídea
Gossypium barbadense	Galápagos cotton	Algodón
Ipomoea habeliana	Lava morning glory	Soguilla
Jasminocereus thouarsii	Candelabra cactus	Cacto, Cirio
Lantana peduncularis	Lantana	Lantana, Supi-rosa
Lecocarpus pinnatifidus	Cutleaf daisy	Lecocarpus
Lycium minimum	Desert thorn	Lycium
Macraea laricifolia	Macraea	Romerillo
Miconia robinsoniana	Miconia	Cacaotillo
Mollugo spp	Carpetweed	Molugo
Nolana galapagensis	Clubleaf	Nolana galápagos
Opuntia spp	Prickly pear cactus	Tuna
Passiflora foetida	Passion flower	Flor de la pasión, Bedoca
Pisonia floribunda	Pega-pega	Pega-pega
Polygola sancti-georgi	Galápagos milkwort	Polygola
Psidium galapageium	Galápagos guava	Guayaba
Scalesia pedunculata	Lechoso	Lechoso
Scalesia spp	Scalesia – 'daisy tree'	Lechoso
Solanum cheesmaniae	Galápagos tomato	Tomatillo
Tillandsia insularis	Bromeliad	Huicundu
Tiquilia nesiotica	Grey matplant	Tiquilia
Tournefortia pubescens	Tournefortia	Turnefortia
Terrestrial invertebrates	Terrestrial invertebrates	Invertebrados terrestres
Agraulis vanillae galapagensis	Silver fritillary butterfly	Mariposa plateada
Camponutus spp	Carpenter ant	Hormiga carpintera
Centruroides exsul	Endemic scorpion	Escorpión endémico
Galapagia solitaria	Praying mantis	Mantis religiosa
Latrodectus apicalis	Endemic black widow	Viuda negra
Leptotes parrhasioides	Galápagos blue butterfly	Mariposa azul
Phoebis sennae	Sulphur butterfly	Mariposa de azufre
Schistocerca melanocera	Painted locust	Saltamonte
Scolopentra galapagoensis	Centipede	Cienpiés
Xylocopa darwinii	Carpenter bee	Abeja carpintera
Reptiles	Reptiles	Reptiles
Amblyrhynchus cristatus	Marine iguana	Iguana marina
Conolophus pallidus	Santa Fe land iguana	Iguana terrestre
Conolophus subcristatus	Galápagos land iguana	Iguana terrestre galapagueña
Geochelone elephantopus	Giant tortoise	Tortuga gigante
Microlophus spp	Lava lizard	Lagartija de lava
Philodryas spp, Alsophis spp	Galápagos snake	Culebra de Galápagos
Phyllodactylus spp	Gecko (some endemic species)	Salamanquesa